## DATE DUE
### Unless Recalled Earlier

| | | | |
|---|---|---|---|
| | | | |
| | | | |
| | | | |
| | | | |
| | | | |
| | | | |
| | | | |
| | | | |
| | | | |
| | | | |
| | | | |
| | | | |
| | | | |
| | | | |
| | | | |
| | | | |
| | | | |
| | | | |

Demco, Inc. 38-293

AMERICA AND THE CRISIS OF WORLD CAPITALISM

*To Gaby*

with my gratitude
for help, sustenance, perceptive criticism,
and *much* more

# AMERICA
# AND THE CRISIS OF
# WORLD CAPITALISM

## JOYCE KOLKO

 BEACON PRESS   *BOSTON*

Copyright © 1974 by Joyce Kolko

Beacon Press books are published under the auspices
of the Unitarian Universalist Association

Published simultaneously in Canada by Saunders of Toronto, Ltd.

Printed in the United States of America

9 8 7 6 5 4 3 2 1

Library of Congress Cataloging in Publication Data

Kolko, Joyce.
    America and the crisis of world capitalism.
    Includes bibliographical references.
    1. United States—Economic conditions—1945-
2. Economic history—1945-   3. International
economic relations.   I. Title.
HC106.5.K538    382.1    74-253
ISBN 0-8070-4790-2

# CONTENTS

# INTRODUCTION

Economics is less "the dismal science" than the bedrock of the social system jealously guarded by the dismal scientists. There are still economists who, clothed in the aura of expertise and technical terminology, take the fundamental facts and relationships that shape the lives of us all and render them either irrelevant or incomprehensible. But there is no reason that a discussion of economic relationships be obtuse, and rather than dull, the subject carries the compelling interest that only the most fundamental aspects of human life provide. For discussions of the world economy relate to war and peace, the class structure, social upheaval, exploitation, revolutionary struggle, suffering and opulence, and all these in turn generate reactions in the economic system. It is, therefore, for all who wish to understand the current world crises, not only economic but political and social as well, to explore the dynamics in the contemporary world economy.

To discuss the world economy is to discuss the capitalist system which is the framework, in the most penetrating and pervasive sense, of economic and political life around the world. And the characteristics of that system have changed much less over the past 75 years than frequently proclaimed. While there have been major shifts in power from industry to industry, or from nation to nation, the purposes and motivating forces of the system have been largely constant. It is my contention that these basic motivations and these consistent operating dynamics are the origins of the contemporary crises. Too many studies, even from the Left, have elaborated theories of neo-capitalism, introducing an array of concepts from the new behavioral sciences, and have, together with the propagandists of the multinational corporations, nearly eliminated even profit as a motivation in capitalist economic behavior.

Before exploring some problems of the international political economy, therefore, we must focus first and foremost on the most simple and obvious features of capitalism: the pursuit of profit, the working class as a commodity in the production process, and the fact that capitalism cannot be successfully planned and the attempts to do so by orthodox economics only generate new crises through the inexorable competitive struggle between company and company, industry and industry, nation and nation as capitalist states move to defend their most powerful sector. And despite the colorful actors that people the stage, despite the incalculable tragedy and death that its operations entail, capitalism is an extremely impersonal system. It is less a perverse machination or even a grand design than each one moving for himself to protect or expand his own interests and profits. No one wants war, depression, inflation, and all the other accompanying crises. These calamities are ultimately the outcome of reflexive acts to protect individual and then national and class interests. Bearing in mind these intrinsic and irreducible features, not only do most of the events of the contemporary crisis come into clearer focus, but so too does the solution.

While the ideological fog of intellectuals celebrating this new capitalism may obscure perception, the reality is there, lived by the vast majority of the world's population, and the dynamics inherent in the system of world capitalism continue to operate. The obscurity is the product of the bourgeoisie who, except during the most severe breakdown of the system, perceive the reality only vicariously through the printed word.

While the major features of capitalism, of course, characterize all capitalist states, and while there has been considerable shifting over the past two decades in its position of power, the United States remains the dominant factor in the world economy and the economic and political developments that emanate from it have had the preeminent influence on the structure elsewhere.

But in presenting an analysis of the American economy in contemporary world capitalism, it is impossible to anchor a discussion to a few months or years which may reflect prosperity at one moment and a severe recession six months later, to be followed by an "upswing" in economic activity within an equally short period of time. Events in the unstable world economy can move swiftly from an era of subjective confidence in profitability to one of crisis and depression. Yet as Paul Mattick emphasized,

> Capital stagnation cannot have physical causes, for the existing material forces of production [labor force and physical plant] are not altered by the crisis. Nor can it find its cause in a material overproduction . . . for in this respect the world is obviously undercapitalized; not enough means of production exist to satisfy even the minimal needs of the world's population. [1]

It is essential, therefore, to pinpoint the underlying structural problems which reemerge with ever-increasing severity, or depend on the escalation of death and destruction in one part of the globe to cast an illusion of prosperity in the other. The motor force of the capitalist system creates, as well as responds to, the political decisions throughout the world. In a world where perpetual oppression and plunder lead to conflict throughout the globe, the U.S. does not have to start or manufacture a war; it merely has to react to conflict in one way or another. And this response will depend as often as not on the economic environment in which it finds itself. Recession, inflation, an "overexpanded" or a stagnating economy, or the fears of such conditions in the minds of men of power, are never the *cause* of direct foreign military interventions or wars. However, the general economic environment and the key decision-makers' concerns about it can set limits on policy options or give greater freedom to policies based on other considerations and judgments. The general economic context also may determine if there will be opposition among the powerful to decisions which may rest directly on other noneconomic calculations. In other words, if a political crisis occurs in one part of the globe when the economy in general is in a slump or recession, political de-

cisions for massive intervention meet with little resistance
and industry actively seeks to profit from new government
orders inherent in large-scale military involvement. Without doubt there never is an explicit decision to start a war
to pull the economy out of a recession. There is simply an
economic environment which encourages, or does not discourage, an expansion of conflict. The Korean war, for
example, would have been a very different conflict had it
started at a time of an inflationary, expansionary world
economy with high "effective" demand for U.S. goods and
services. But the very processes of war create, in addition
to the intolerable horror for millions, further economic
pressures undermining the entire system over the long run.

Although the nature of decision-making has been
meticulously examined by many earlier studies, in a society
rift by conflicting interests, clearly an analysis that is obvious to some is contentious to others. Certain assumptions,
such as the nature of the ruling class, the role of ideology,
and the process of decision-making, underlie this study and
have guided my analysis.

For bourgeois economists there is no need for an
understanding of a ruling class or, often, even the intrusion
of political events into their studies of growth, development, finance, and the like. Capitalism is the "given" in
the sense of the physical environment and they either advocate the operations of its "laws" with as little restraint
as possible or they wish to modify or humanize the system
with government welfare measures and fiscal policies. But
they still compartmentalize economics from other aspects
of society, such as the political and social dimension, which
is defined separately in the advanced industrial states as
"liberal democracy."

For others, of course, capitalism is the defining social
system whose operations touch every aspect of life, one
that is organized into an obvious class structure of irrecon-
cilable interests, and for whom imperialism is more than
the domination of one state by another or by foreign corporate interests but is also the imposition of a social system.

In the metamorphosis of words from analytic tools

to political slogans, considerable confusion as to the reality of such terms as "ruling class," "imperialism," "empire," can evolve. I assume that the ruling class in the capitalist states is the capitalist class. The ultimate decisions are not shared by elites such as the military or the "mandarins" which, like the police and politicians, are only servants of the ruling class. And it is misleading to divide the ruling class into financial-industrial-geographic cliques. Nor is there a conspiracy of the ruling class to preserve the "empire," nor is it helpful to isolate the state from the capitalist system in discussions of imperialism. A fashionable and pseudo-sophisticated notion of the Left is that the ruling class in America is now divided into two regional-industrial cliques — the Eastern Rockefeller Establishment challenged by the banking-industrial group of the Southwest — struggling with each other for the control of political power. Such simplistic conceptualizations, both analytically and empirically, confuse rather than clarify the process of decision-making in America. For instance, linking Nixon to a "Southwest industrial-banking clique" as opposed to an "Eastern Rockefeller clique" seriously distorts analysis and overlooks the obvious empirical fact that when Nixon introduced deflationary policies in 1969-70 through a cutback in Pentagon orders, they fell first and hardest on the industries in the Southwest. Within the U.S. capitalist class the division historically is between trade-oriented industries and the protectionist interests, and this continues to be the major division. But within these categories the conflict is intense between individual interests whenever they collide.

There is nothing mystical, or even ideological, about the decisions of the ruling class, nor its disagreements. Their aim is not even to expand the "Empire" of *American* power per se. Their aim is, and must be, to expand their own corporate interests. Most members of the ruling class do not generally articulate their political power or even conceive of themselves as other than "citizens" on general issues of society, including war and peace. And, if disassociated from their economic role, this may well be the case. It is in their relationship to their direct economic interests that they act unhesitatingly as political men of power and influence. Capitalists in individual corporations must, and do, consider only the interests of their corporation. When they leave the corporation for a government post they must consider the whole environment for collective corporate action in general. But their day-to-day activities will again largely deal with the interests of specific industries. Only rarely do they have the leisure or inclination to take the grand view, other than the unquestioned assumptions that underlie the actions of all capitalist decision-makers, which are so accepted as to require no contemplation. The grand view, beyond clichés, is often projected on them later. This explains in part the incredulity of decision-makers as they read historical assessments of their role. But despite the desire of academics to find every other motivation for government decision-making, particularly in foreign policy, one need only casually scan the *Department State Bulletin,* the organ not of the Commerce Department but of foreign policy, to find that the vast majority of the topics discussed are economic and the groups addressed are businessmen.

Throughout this book I refer to the dominant sector of the American ruling class, which can best be defined as the executives of the top 50 to 100 industrial and banking corporations who have consolidated more than one-half of America's industrial and financial power in the world. The role of the state is, on the whole, to promote the welfare of the most powerful sector and to respond to specific interests on concrete issues. When the two are in conflict, the most powerful generally prevail. But by the time the dominant sector has asserted its influence much has often transpired over the specific issues and a crisis may be in process, requiring new responses and actions. This process is dynamic and not susceptible to tidy formulas of regional interests. This is not to say, however, that it is "accident" prone, or that decisions are made in a haphazard manner or on an ideological basis. For decisions respond to material needs of the ruling capitalist class, and there is much jockeying for advantage when interests conflict, which they do, not as regional cliques but between profit-oriented individual corporate interests. Yet the dominant sector does not give orders to the state in an authoritarian context. There are too many conflicts of interest among them to operate in this fashion. Only with a real threat from the Left do capitalist factions unite to support totalitarian rule.

Throughout this study I assume that material interests, and not ideology, are the basis for economic and political decisions. If the materialist explanations for all historical events are not readily apparent, I assume that all the evidence is not yet available and do not seek ideological causes, any more than a scientist will substitute mystical explanations for unknown phenomena. There are countless examples of ideological explanations, either out of ignorance of the material interests or for ulterior motives, describing everything from the origins of World War I to the most recent local wars. Ideology is the mask over the face of material interests. It is used to manipulate the people but never really penetrates the rulers, who may discard it when it no longer serves their purposes. With such a perspective there need be no surprise or confusion regarding the "détente" after years of the "Cold War." Such a shift involves no trauma for the rulers but only for the ideologues and the mandarins who serviced their earlier needs. For the ruling classes, the practical men-of-affairs, it is a matter of material interest and a new ideology can be molded to fit new needs.

For a number of years discussions of the world economy, from the monetary crisis, the multinationals, or the energy "crisis," to the balance-of-payments and trade deficits, have left the financial pages and the business press and have become issues of popular attention and concern. Economists are consulted as oracles to predict future developments. Yet more important than predictions is to grasp the dynamics at work and the integration of the seemingly disparate aspects of the political economy. What is the nature of the monetary crisis and the signifi-

cance of the Eurodollar in the instability? How did it
evolve and why? What was the impact of the Vietnam
war on the world economy, and the effects of the economy
on the war? What is the full significance of the new giant
corporations, the "multinationals," on the world capitalist
structure?

For years after World War II the United States was
the unchallenged superpower of the capitalist world, but
now it is apparent that Europe and Japan rival its pretensions. What was the origin of that shift in relative standing
and how secure is the strength of the new powers? In the
past the capitalist states have struggled for markets and
raw materials throughout the world and their conflict has
led to global conflagrations. It is critical to examine their
current conflict in trade in relation to the other developments in the economy. Of basic importance is the nature
of class conflicts that economic developments can generate
and the role of the working class in the industrial economies
at the present time. Intimately linked to the condition of
the industrial capitalist states is the fate of the Third World.
What has been the impact of the two decades of "development" in the vast preindustrial regions of the world, and,
in turn, what is the potential of the Third World to modify
the crisis in industrial capitalism? And now, after decades
of quarantine, how must we assess the impact of the integration of the Soviet bloc and China on the longevity of
world capitalism?

These and similar questions are in fact intimately
interrelated and provide the focus of this brief volume.
If I do not presume to provide all the answers I have tried
to restrict this book to those few essential problems of
America and the world capitalist crisis, and to make the
discussion as succinct as possible. Clearly, a comprehensive account of so broad a topic could run into thousands
of pages. It is my hope that here I can at least raise some
important questions of the political economy and to
ascertain new pressures toward crisis or consolidation.

### CHAPTER ONE

# THE UNITED STATES AND THE WORLD ECONOMY: AN OVERVIEW OF TWO DECADES

To unravel causal factors for momentous events in history, much less predict the specific forms and times of crisis, is an awesome task even if one possesses a detailed conceptual and factual understanding of the operations of the capitalist system. There are, indeed, a multitude of interacting forces that can produce very different responses from those who hold the reins of power either in the state, the economy, or both. It is this interplay of innumerable and contradictory elements rather than control and order that is one of the defining features of world capitalism. But to evaluate all the factors at play in the world economy over the past two decades would be an insuperable task. In this chapter, then, I wish merely to sketch in the broadest outline some of the developments of the post-Korean war economy and to emphasize in more detail the political and economic events and interactions of the past five years. These interactions, which constitute a pattern that has defined the present environment for world economic activity, are in large part shaped by the responses of various key capitalist states to fluctuations in the so-called business cycle.

## 1954-1964

Such a cursory discussion of some of the economic interactions between the government and the business cycle in no way captures the true nature of the decade between the Korean and Indochina wars. If that decade pales beside the subsequent years of unprecedented violence in Vietnam, it still contained its own share of brutal suppression. Beyond the daily, unpublicized exploitation that is the lot, in varying degrees, of the vast majority of the agricultural and industrial workers around the world, there was violent and sustained repression in such areas as Vietnam, Guatemala, Malaysia, the Congo, the Middle East, the Philippines, Korea, Brazil, and Algeria.

In America it was also a decade of intellectual consensus and complacency that celebrated, from the historical perspective of ten years, not only the resilience of capitalism but its beneficence as well, and this perspective was coupled with a fervent, and functional, anticommunism. That ideology was the ostensible justification for the vast export of dollars to Europe and Japan known as "offshore procurement" and "defense support," and for the stationing of troops overseas whose expenses eventually contributed billions to local economies and promoted their recovery, growth, and demand for U.S. goods and services. The supply of money created to make this vast expansion of the world economy possible continued for four years after the Korean war, and U.S. budget and payments deficits and inflation increased each year. The Korean war provoked growth in the American economy that continued through 1956, when the gross national product (GNP) was 25 percent greater than in 1950. Many industries, such as aluminum, more than doubled their output in the years between 1950 and 1955. Domestically, an investment boom in 1955-56 reflected Washington's continued expansionary fiscal and monetary policy, heavy military spending, and an export surplus. During these years there was a strong demand on American productive capacity from both the public and private sectors in the U.S. as well as abroad.

In 1957 the American government, alarmed over the persistent inflation and budget and international payments deficits, decided to take steps to curb the expansionary boom via the traditional means of strong restrictions on the credit supply and a sharp cutback in defense spending. As the Federal Reserve Bank raised interest rates, the Defense Department abruptly told its largest 25 suppliers that it could no longer pay for existing orders, let alone place new ones. Meanwhile, the tight money policy restricted loans, leaving many firms with no alternatives to the cancelled orders. These political decisions only hastened the forces, such as falling profitability, already operating in the economy. And in fact the decisions were not made capriciously, but because the Administration understood that there was a crisis in the operation of the economy. It was a traditional, if precipitous, effort to curtail the enormous demand for credit, not only from the private corporations but from the government itself. It appeared to those running the Federal Reserve System that decisive action was needed to curb the inflationary boom. The outcome was near panic and a recession in 1957-58. Unemployment rose to 7.5 percent and production fell sharply — 27 percent in durables, and 40 percent in autos and steel, between April 1957 and April 1958.

In late 1958, under pressure from an alarmed business community, the government then articulated a new policy around a feigned "sputnik crisis," and introduced stimulative spending measures — primarily increased military spending — and raised the budget deficit from $2.8 billion to $12.4 billion. The mini-boom was also supported by renewed industrial inventory stockpiling, which made up 60 percent of the increase in the GNP. The government, once more alarmed by the deficit, during 1959 again sharply restrained credit and the money supply, producing a new recession in 1960. Simultaneously, the economy's problems were accentuated by a massive flight of U.S. capital to Europe.[1]

In certain regions of the U.S. the 1958 recession could be more aptly defined as a depression. The auto industry and dependent companies were particularly hard hit, with unemployment in Detroit of 12.5 percent. This experience, the worst since the 1930s, guaranteed that union leaders would join the company executives in Washington begging Congress for more arms contracts during the early years of the Vietnam war. Unemployment throughout the U.S. never dropped below 5.5 percent during the "recovery" period of 1959-64.

After seven years of boom in the economy triggered by the Korean war, the recession seriously shook the confidence of many American capitalists. But equally important, the West European nations, in a decision reflecting their new strength and confidence, made their currencies convertible into the dollar when they established the European Economic Community (EEC) in 1958. For American business, this step provided the means for entering the more profitable and expanding European market and for repatriating their profits, while the recession at home provided an added incentive. The result was that the period 1958-64 saw the greatest expansion in American foreign investment.[2]

### 1964-1974

The Vietnam war was indisputably the major stimulus of the economic boom between 1964 and 1968, and during that time the entire economy reaped immense profits. The vast increase in government and then consumer demand led to relatively high employment and a substantial and careless expansion in both corporate and consumer credit based on new confidence in an expanding economy. Profits, wages, and prices all rose to new heights. As in 1950, there was an "anticipation" boom after the escalation in 1965, with excessive inventory accumulations. The "real" gross national product, after deducting for inflation, grew at an annual rate of 6 percent. U.S. industries, satisfied with government orders and the fallout of a growing aggregate consumer demand, were less and less concerned about their export markets and competitive imports. And as U.S. prices mounted and the delivery-time of American industry was prolonged, orders for consumer goods and industrial supplies were increasingly placed with foreign competitors in Europe and Japan, repeating a pattern that occurred during the Korean war and which accounted for the German and Japanese economic "miracles." Imports of manufactured goods rose from 35 percent of total imports in 1960 to 55 percent by 1969. Some American industries were hurt during these years, particularly certain sectors of agriculture, but, by and large, with the expansive boom the market was big enough for everyone. Meanwhile, however, the accompanying domestic inflation was eroding the value of the dollar — with grave implications for the future. The cost of the war was financed through greatly expanded deficit spending, since it was politically too unpopular to try to fund with increased taxation. Furthermore, in 1965, the first year of massive ground forces involvement in Indochina, McNamara made his famous underestimation of the war costs for the 1967 budget by $10 billion, an error of 100 percent. The result of these compounded events was that between 1965 and 1969 the dollar lost 19 percent of its value. During these same years U.S. merchandise exports fell from their 1960-64 average of $5.4 billion to $2.8 billion.[3]

The immensely profitable and stimulating nature of the war for the whole economy between 1964 and 1968 often prompted newspapers to headline sharp drops in Wall Street as the result of "peace scares" during abortive diplomatic moves. It is important to understand that the "peace scares" did not mean that businessmen, in general, encouraged or discouraged the war. When the stock market fell or business lobbied for defense contracts it was not because the U.S. capitalists were committed to fighting in Vietnam per se, but rather they wished to avoid immediate loss by selling stocks likely to fall with an end to the conflict, or to gain from the profits of government contracts. The whole conflict, from their point of view, was impersonal and their action was based on the simple criterion of profit and loss. When, on the other hand, the war actually could be pinpointed as threatening present or future profits, they would act politically to try to reduce its costs. It is important to remember the difference to the general economy between military spending that may entail a huge military budget, with emphasis on strategic arms and sophisticated weapon systems, and a war economy. The former can be seen as vertical spending — heavy on technology, high salaries for skilled scientists and engineers, and high profits for a few companies. The weapons are limited in number and not intended to be used. In a war economy, on the other hand, the same direct expenditure will have a horizontal effect across the whole economy, especially when large numbers of troops are involved. Hundreds of thousands of weapons and supplies — from paper cups to helicopters, from uniforms to ammunition — are all consumed and replaced. All these direct expenditures, in turn, require massive purchases of steel, textiles, paper, and the like. The large numbers of workers, employed for wages in direct production for the war, in turn create demand for goods and services. This multiplying and expansive effect had a decisive impact on the economies around the world. Strategic weapons research and development, by contrast, affects relatively few industries and workers, is therefore more acceptable in an inflationary economy, and is primarily a subsidy to specific industries.

By 1968, the inflation generated by the war had become counterproductive to the overall American economy. The most powerful U.S. industrialists saw the writing on the wall in the form of monetary crises, payments deficits, blocks on capital flow, a growing hostility to their investments in Europe, competitive loss of markets, and especially the rapid loss of the value of the dollar. In sum, except for a few industries, the war in a few years became a distinct liability to the overall economy and to future profits. The monetary crisis of the spring of 1968 clearly underlined the weakness of the dollar. The U. S. Treasury lost $1.4 billion in gold over the first quarter of that year, straining the old gold-exchange system to the point where the major capitalist governments agreed to a two-tiered gold market whereby the U.S. would sell gold only to the central banks at the fixed price of $35 an ounce. The European bankers also called for a change in the Vietnam policies and economic "discipline" in the domestic economy. But this March agreement provided only a very temporary respite. It was this pressure from key U.S. capitalists, in coordination with European bankers, which in March 1968 forced a pause in Washington's escalation policies and Johnson's withdrawal from the Presidential election. The military factor of the Tet offensive was also decisive in convincing these same elements that the Vietnamese were far from defeated and the costly, seemingly peripheral, war could prove interminable.

Since at least the beginning of 1968 the attitude of the dominant sector of the American capitalists toward the Vietnam war has been mercurial. For that sector with an overall concern for the American economy, trade, and investment abroad, broad questions of inflation, value of money, and the like will variously be an active or a passive force in policymaking. In 1968, regarding the war, it was extremely active; in 1969-70 it was passive; in 1971, active; and in 1972, again passive. Each time their position reflected the condition of the general economy, as I noted in the Introduction. When this dominant sector is passive the specific interests whose fortunes and fate are directly linked to continued war or its outcome, come to the fore and their pressures influence decision-making. The oil companies, of course, would prefer a friendly puppet granting them concessions, if possible, but the war in Vietnam was never fought with tin or oil as *the* cause. It would be surely more beneficial, say, to overthrow Quadaffi than to fight in Vietnam for still unknown oil reserves. But the oil corporations are likely to encourage American efforts in Vietnam once the possibilities of achieving their concessions, let alone oil, became clear.

The Nixon Administration in 1969, in part, responded to the hostility to a prolonged and expensive war, intending both to secure military victory in Vietnam and, at the same time, to reduce internal inflation and the balance-of-payments deficit. Hoping to neutralize its powerful critics, the Administration introduced a limited phased withdrawal of troops from Vietnam, the most inflationary aspect of the war, as well as the most visible to Americans, and put its effort behind orthodox deflationary policies to control inflation. There is no doubt that these moves toward a shift in policy direction relieved some pressure for a short period from that sector of

American capitalists opposed to the war, but the new mone-
tarist policies quickly set in motion another succession of
disastrous consequences. But pointing out that a shift in
military policy in Vietnam from U.S. troops to bombers,
artillery, the so-called electronic warfare, and, illusively,
"Vietnamization," theoretically was removing the inflationary
aspect of the war does not exhaust the reasons for the troop
withdrawal. The political motivations were obvious, as was
the fact that the troops were simply not militarily effective,
and this, of course, added to their inflationary potential.
Removal of the troops and the simultaneous reduction of
government war orders for aircraft, weapons, ammunition,
fuel, food, and clothing were deflationary moves even if inflation continued. By May 1970, according to the business press,
"cutbacks in military and space spending have left the industry mired in its own private depression . . . ."[4]

In 1969 the Nixon Administration also introduced the
traditional monetary deflationary policies of a sharply
restricted money supply and high interest rates intended to
slow economic expansion, to cut consumer purchasing power
by increasing unemployment, and perhaps attract some flow
of dollars from abroad. Both the European and American
bankers and economists had been calling for such "disciplinary" measures to control American inflation for some years,
but they generally also included a termination of the Indochina war. The results, while fully predictable by anyone
who understands the real workings of the capitalist system,
especially the introduction of the planless "planning" of
orthodox economic theory, were once more unanticipated
by those making the decisions.

After the boom years of vast economic expansion between 1964 and 1969, based in great part on the careless
growth of corporate and consumer credit in turn generated
by war-induced confidence, the introduction of tight money
policies quickly led to an acute liquidity crisis among banks
and large corporations. Municipalities also had borrowed until
the interest rates were beyond their capacities, and, facing a
crisis, they issued bonds in excess. Corporations short of
liquidity massively increased their stock issue in 1969-70 for

an average of between four to six times the average number of earlier years. These issues flooded the market at a time when business confidence was sagging generally. The U.S. banks also faced a liquidity crisis as certificates of deposit (CDs) became due and new deposits declined. During 1969-70 American banks then turned to the Eurodollar market, primarily to their own branches in London, borrowing over $15 billion. This new demand for dollars in the U.S. forced the Eurodollar interest rates up to unprecedented levels, attracting dollars from every quarter of the world for interest rates as high as 12 percent. The dollar reserves in European central banks declined sharply during this period as they themselves fed the voracious market and private holdings increased enormously. U.S. official balance-of-payments settlements were briefly in surplus. Nevertheless, by June 1970 the liquidity crisis had contributed to bankruptcies from the small marginally financed firms that rode the crest of the economic boom years to the Penn Central, the nation's largest railroad.

By the third quarter of 1970 political pressures forced yet another shift in economic policy:  interest rates were lowered progressively and the money supply expanded in order to insure that the nation would not be in the midst of depression at election time in 1972. The *intent* of expanding the money supply and lowering interest rates was to stimulate the economy once more and to lower the rate of unemployment. *In fact,* of course, lowering the interest rates sent a flood of dollars out of the country as banks acted to repay the high interest Eurodollar loans. Others, lacking confidence in the American economy, sought the high interest rates obtainable in other currencies. As Eurodollar interest rates fell sharply with the drop in U.S. demand, private holders turned their dollars into the European central banks for more profitable currencies. Central bank dollar reserves began to swell during the third quarter of 1970 from $10 to $20 billion, an increase equal to U.S. gold reserves, and the international monetary crisis began anew.

By November 1970 the only encouraging statistic in the U.S. economy for the Nixon Administration was the fall in interest rates.  Other indicators revealed both persisting inflation, growing unemployment, and business stagnation in the critical areas of profits, investment, orders, inventories, and the like.  And although Richard Nixon understands nothing about economics he clearly understood that such economic statistics, plus a continued war in Vietnam, would spell defeat for his political ambitions in 1972.

With the deflationary restrictions in the U.S. economy in 1970, U.S. industry, relatively indifferent over the past boom years to the increased imports, began to press once more for protection against lower-cost imported cars, textiles, steel, and such.  Any industry with a slack in demand and mounting inventories will invariably advocate protectionist policies.  Under these conditions trade conflict with the other capitalist states is inevitable, and has a self-perpetuating character.

During 1970 there was also considerable agitation in Congress for high tariff legislation, in particular curbs on the imports of textiles, shoes, and steel.  The Europeans, in turn, began to examine the possibilities of retaliation.  In the fall of 1970 Congress nearly passed a protectionist trade bill that would have triggered immediate foreign reaction. European industries presented a collective official warning to U.S. ambassadors in November.  The British government, for its part, initiated studies as to where retaliation would inflict the greatest pain on the U.S.  It concluded that while transport, industrial equipment, and grains were vulnerable, it was primarily soybeans, America's biggest export to Europe with a trade of $600 million in fiscal 1970, that they could attack most easily.

The trade bill aroused the intense ire of the American foreign trade-oriented business elite as well, enough to convince an Administration initially sympathetic to protectionism that other means would have to be found to develop an American trade advantage.  The major alternative became an effort to force the upward revaluation of the European and Japanese currencies.

The 1969-71 U.S. recession began to shape the course of events on the other side of the Atlantic by November

1970. The European governments had begun to introduce deflationary policies to control inflation, but since it was stimulated by the massive infusion of foreign capital during the monetary crisis, they were effectively unable to do so. The result, according to one German banker, was the ". . .worst of two worlds, an economic slowdown and rising prices."[5] Since both Japan and Germany had geared their production to export, particularly to the U.S., their own internal demand was "soft or softening." Meanwhile, U.S. corporations hoped that they could expand their own exports to Europe to compensate for the lack of orders at home. Predictably, the same attitude became stronger among the European capitalists.

Nixon, who found such economic problems bewildering, finally responded viscerally when, at the end of 1970, his advisers explained that the U.S. would soon be a third-rate power in world trade. Reportedly, he was "bowled over," and his traditional response was to get "tough."[6] But the new toughened trade diplomacy, expected to lead to an "anything goes" policy in international trade competition, rested on the assumption that the U.S. could continue to play the role of the sole capitalist superpower.

Pressures of a more immediate sort were mounting on the Administration from all sides by the end of 1970. In keeping with its arrogant posture, even in a position of growing objective weakness, the Administration made the decision at the end of the year that others would continue to pay for American policies. Declaring himself now "a Keynesian," Nixon embarked in 1971 on a thoroughgoing effort to salvage the American economy in time for the election. In a sharp reversal of his earlier tight money policy, the rate of money growth was expanded in the first quarter of 1971 by 10.8 percent, higher than any time since 1950, in order to induce new investments in the U.S. for jobs and prosperity. But instead the new dollars continued to flow out of the U.S. and into the European central banks.

The government maintained its cavalier stance in face of growing European hostility to the inflow of dollars. The report of the Council of Economic Advisers (CEA) declared

in mid-February 1971 that the U.S. had no intention of
shaping the domestic economy to please foreign countries.
If these nations worried about the deluge of dollars or U.S.
inflation, the Administration suggested, the Europeans
should revalue their currencies upward more often.  The
European bankers and politicians then confronted the fact
that Washington intended to use its skyrocketing balance-of-
payments deficit as a tool to force them to pay the costly
price, in the form of trade losses and recession, for American
domestic and international policies.  The crisis was underlined in February 1971 as $800 million poured into the
German Bundesbank during the last week and an additional
flood of dollars moved into other central banks.

Further emphasizing his lack of concern over international economic questions, Nixon created greater alarm,
not only among the Europeans but the American banking
community as well, by appointing John Connally as Secretary of the Treasury.  Connally reputedly had absolutely no
understanding of economic questions but instead had a vis-
ceral and jingoistic belief in America's omnipotence in the
world.  Further exposing the Administration's intent and
aggravating the mounting tensions abroad during the same
month was the comment by Gottfried Haebler, the Harvard
economist and adviser to Nixon, that the U.S. should treat
its payments deficit with "benign neglect."  The European
response was to ask for Washington's gold in exchange for
dollars, and they increasingly accused the U.S. of "a lack
of seriousness" in regard to the dollar and the world monetary structure. [7]

In early April 1971, in an attempt to stem the flow of
dollars through the Eurodollar market, the Europeans asked
the U.S. to increase its short-term interest rates.  Connally
opposed the move and in fact further lowered the rates, and
the European central banks were forced to begin to cut their
own rates in April to deter the flow of dollars.  Despite this
move, in mid-April a deluge of dollars forced the printing of
new marks to buy the dollars and increased the German
money supply by an annual rate of 22 percent.  As the pres-

sure increased on Washington, Arthur Burns rather lamely asserted that the U.S. was indeed concerned about its balance-of-payments. But concrete actions convinced everyone that the Administration had no intention of yielding to international pressure; and under the existing system the deficit would continue to grow — and with it the Europeans would continue to pay for American expansion at the expense of their own economies.

On May 5 the Germans floated the mark after taking in $1 billion in one hour, and a total of over $5 billion during the first four months of 1971. Repercussions followed quickly across Europe, with many other nations floating their currencies or revaluing as central banks refused to support the American currency at the old parity. Only France prevented the *de facto* revaluation of all European currencies relative to the dollar. The political impact on the EEC of this unilateral German move was profound, and I later discuss its implications. In Washington there was total silence during the early days of the May crisis. As one aide remarked caustically, "Neither Nixon nor Connally understand this sort of thing."[8] But there was in fact more than ignorance involved. On May 10, in the midst of the crisis, the Treasury announced that the situation required "no immediate action" by the U.S. The *Wall Street Journal* saw the government more intent on forcing changes internationally than in the domestic economy. The Administration was not going to "put the U.S. economy through the wringer" to handle the "temporary" international crisis, Vice President Agnew declared.[9] The Europeans read the message and between May 3 and 11 asked for $422 million in gold, reducing the American stock to $10.6 billion.

By June 1971 the new statistics and mounting alarm from the critical sector of the American ruling class revealed the full impact of failure on every front to the Administration. It was evident that the U.S. would face its first acknowledged balance-of-trade deficit in the twentieth century. In announcing the deficit, Secretary of Commerce Stans also pointed out that the U.S. needed a $4-5 billion surplus in trade to counteract the losses due to military expenditures and capital outflow for foreign investment. In addition, what the economists had come to term "stagflation" characterized the domestic economy; business activity was stagnating — reflecting a total failure of the so-called "stimulative" measures (except insofar as they stimulated a world monetary crisis) simultaneously with continued rapid inflation. By June monetary reserves were the lowest since 1938. In mid-June, the Swiss turned in $50 million for gold, bringing their year's request to $125 million. The U.S. had exhausted most of its borrowing rights with the International Monetary Fund (IMF), which now refused to accept any nation's dollars as payment of debts, for its dollar quota was filled. And to pay its debts abroad the U.S. government borrowed foreign currencies at high interest rates. In 1969 U.S. total interest and dividend payments abroad reached $5 billion, and they were certain to rise over the following years.

During July the economic statistics continued to weaken and it was evident that the Administration's budget deficit would set a record at $23.2 billion that would be at least double the estimate of January. And as the dollar outflow, spurred by these very bleak statistics, accelerated despite the floating currencies, the Administration had to assess its course. Its options by this time were extremely limited and actively discussed by many European and American economists. Characteristically, the Americans chose to try once more to mask their weakness by bluffing. A rude, tough diplomatic offensive on the economic front was calculated policy. Connally was only the most colorful and obvious example. "We've been good saps, but that era has ended," one key U.S. negotiator blurted out to his stunned European counterpart in May.[10] At another negotiating session with Common Market diplomats, the President's trade envoy, William Eberle, during an important discussion, turned to one negotiator and told him, "I don't like people who nod their heads. . . ." The Europeans, rankled, termed him "obnoxious" and "an insult."[11] Such a style had distinct political purposes, and even if it would finally prove counter-productive, the options were hardly more acceptable to Washington. It was not going to acknowledge its reduced relative power and reassess its global strategy in light of this fact.

The approaching crisis in the U.S. and world capitalist economies, so evident by July 1971, and the cavalier and vacillating approach of the Administration, finally brought the full pressure of the most powerful American business interests to play in the direct formulation of policy. The politically inspired steel settlement of early August angered the bulk of business interests as it pointed to continued un-controlled inflation. It also demonstrated Nixon's over-weening desire to seek expedient political advantages by courting favor of a few at the expense of the economic needs of the entire system. "A lot of us are getting scared," de-clared one executive who reflected the alarm of many. Business in general regarded some kind of government wage-price controls as mandatory "to bring us down to earth again." During July, according to one government econo-mist assigned to take them, such worried and angry calls on the state of the economy to the Administration had been "an absolute debacle."[12]

Incorporating most of the anxieties and demands of the world-oriented American corporations on the direction of the economy was the report of the President's Commis-sion on International Trade and Investment Policy, appointed in September 1970. Headed by Albert Williams, former president of IBM, the commission presented its 400-page report to Nixon in July 1971. It advised a temporary import surcharge, a change of currency parities, wage and price con-trols, negotiations to eliminate trade barriers — in short, it outlined Nixon's August 15, 1971, speech overturning the existing international monetary system. A critical aspect of that speech was that the Administration gave no advance warning to any foreign government as to the timing or extent of the move.

The blitzkrieg approach of ultimatums and no consultation with the other capitalist states was partially designed to mask the crisis in the U.S. economy. Consultations involve negotiations, threats of reprisals, demands for concessions, and the like from others. Unilateral fiat, on the other hand, presents the shock of recognizing a powerful and unreasonable adversary, one apparently quite willing to destroy the entire economic structure if unable to achieve its ends. To respond to such dangers takes more time and careful deliberation to reorganize one's forces. The reaction will be slower but no less definitive. For then the choice to be considered is whether the whole system shall fall or whether others can organize defenses to protect their own interests. A dynamic exists which cannot be overlooked in examining the more cautious reactions of other capitalist states to American unilateral acts. But more than that, each capitalist state must, and will, look after its own needs, in unison if advantageous, or alone.

Following Nixon's August 15 policy statement Connally declared that the surtax was not negotiable nor was the more important question of convertibility. These harsh and crude tactics, again much more calculated policy than the style of a Texan, had decisive long-term political, economic, and strategic significance. The earlier monetary arrangements were no longer advantageous for the U.S., and revaluation of the other currencies was the major goal — thereby, in fact, reducing the national debt. Germany had responded but France and Japan had refused to yield. The calculation of the economists in Washington that the market mechanism would automatically force all the other currencies up further reflected one irrational aspect of capitalist behavior. Moreover, the remedial reforms needed simultaneously to stabilize the dollar and reactivate the economy, expand exports, and provide protection from competitive imports to the threatened domestic industries, were all contradictory.

Nations with a small percentage of their exports aimed at the U.S. market feared that those two countries with a larger proportion — Germany and Japan — would flow into their own markets when blocked by restrictions in the U.S.

The effects of such moves in an integrated system are fully predictable. The major development in world trade over the past decade, particularly in Europe and Japan, has been the expansion of manufactured consumer goods as a percentage of total world trade, and the U.S. was one of the largest markets. This growth, of course, is most susceptible to recession or closing access to a large market and a general fall in aggregate demand, and the potential domino effect of such a decline is obvious.

In Europe, West Germany, with 40 percent of the EEC production and the chief market for its neighbors, was the key to future trends. In August 1971 its leading bankers were predicting a recession as serious as any since World War II, particularly in 1972. Most European bankers recognized that a fall in investment on top of a monetary crisis contained the seeds of a "dangerous situation."[13]  By October 1971 there was full agreement that recessionary forces were in full movement throughout the Common Market. Heavy capital investment was essential to pull out of the stagnation, but so much uncertainty as to the future made it appear extremely unlikely. By November all German corporations polled reported sharp drops in profits and capital spending along with rising production costs. Unemployment, or merely reduction in overtime and an introduction of short time, cut the spending power of the consumer in West Germany. Tensions mounted with the French, who with currency parity changes since 1969 had gained a 30 percent trading advantage. But the French believed the Germans brought their problems on themselves by yielding to American pressure and, without consultation, floating the mark in May 1971.

As their economic climate showed growing signs of recession, the European attitude toward the possibility of a devalued dollar changed, especially in light of the surcharge. While once declaring the dollar's gross overvaluation in regard to U.S. investment power, they now struggled to maintain a parity that would not deal a further recessionary blow to their own economies by making American goods more com-

petitive. The other capitalist governments had no intention
of allowing the money markets full freedom, any more than
the U.S. would allow its reserves to be depleted, and they
intervened actively to control foreign exchanges and capital
flows — and the period was known as the "phony float."
There were no major retaliatory moves to Nixon's fiat of
August 15 due to their fear of recession and their conviction
of the U.S. irrational reactions to any moves on their part.
At the end of August the American negotiators were full of
confidence in their new leverage. The long-term effects could
scarcely be more serious for the future, but, of course, the
alternatives were hardly better. Years of mismanagement
and confused priorities had narrowed the American options
to arrogant threats and unilateral fiats or the abdication of
their unique position in the world economy *vis-à-vis* the
other capitalist states.

Washington followed its August 15 pronouncement
with an ultimatum to the Japanese regarding their textile
exports, thereby securing a "voluntary" quota from Tokyo
but also further seriously straining already tense relations.
This move, largely repaying a political debt to the southern
textile industry, intensified pressures for protection from
the shoe and some electronic industries, the trade unions,
and others affected by competitive imports, further alarming
U.S. foreign-trade interests. The U.S. continued its extrava-
gant demands on the other capitalist powers as if the excessive nature of the demands could somehow make it appear
more powerful than it was in reality. In mid-September
1971 Connally next astounded the Europeans and Japanese
by informing them that the U.S. was "broke" and that they
must act to reverse its balance-of-payments deficit, which
in September was known to be three times the previous
record of 1970, and provide the Americans with a $13 billion
surplus.[14] Then in November, Connally appeared at a Group
of Ten meeting and declared that gold should be demone-
tized. Finally, in December 1971 Washington demanded
that the EEC curtail their grain production and stockpile
their output in order to aid U.S. agricultural sales in Europe.

While seriously aggravating diplomatic relations, wrecking the carefully constructed alliance system, and putting the Western Europeans and Japanese on guard, the immediate economic impact of all these moves was minimal and scarcely achieved the U.S. objectives. Although it applied to 60 percent of the exports of the industrial states to the U.S. and to one-third of those of the Third World, the surtax failed to affect in any decisive way imports into America which remained competitive. This failure, in fact, brought the end of the tax in December. Its only real fruits were greatly increased animosity everywhere. The Europeans continued to move ahead with their plans for the EEC via agreements that would threaten up to $300 million in U.S. exports, as well as to develop or finalize trade agreements with China, Brazil, Argentina, and Uruguay.

The impact of the August 15 policy on the U.S. economy was predictably mercurial. The stock market soared briefly and plunged again in mid-September, but as the weeks passed the more critical economic indicators continued to reveal acute underlying crisis.

U.S. industry by November suddenly became extremely alarmed over the approaching recession in Western Europe as foreclosing their opportunity to pull out of their own slump. The multinational corporations began to revise downward their investment plans in Europe and feared a shrinking of profits and a protectionist wave. With such forces underway, all nations will respond to protect their own economic and political positions. Nixon's moves, while beneficial to certain sectors of American capitalism, were distinctly counterproductive to others. And his erratic behavior in an attempt to satisfy all only aggravated the situation. Internationally he was quite ready to accept the consequences of his policies until Kissinger convinced him in late November that the entire alliance system was in grave danger. This awareness led to the summit meetings with the Western European leaders and the inevitable decision of December 18 to devalue the dollar.[15] At this point, many believed, the American monetary imperium, on which much of its power rested, came to an end, and the combat for economic supremacy among the capitalist states had begun anew. But in fact the economies were too integrated for the devaluation to alter world economic relations so decisively.

## Aftermath of the December Agreement

The decisions of December 18, 1971, provided only a momentary respite and the negotiations themselves provoked new bitterness in international economic relations. By their own criteria, the American moves could strengthen the economic position of the dollar and the U.S. balance-of-payments only if certain measures followed. Chief among these would be a massive reflow of dollars back to the U.S. for profit-taking following the devaluation — $7 to $8 billion were anticipated, according to Arthur Burns.[16]  Furthermore, the Europeans and Japanese expected Washington to pursue certain "disciplinary" deflationary policies to defend its own reserves after devaluation, including an increase in its interest rates and curbs on the flow of capital. These had to accompany an end to the most obvious drain on its resources — the Indochina war. As could have been predicted, none of these measures was forthcoming. In fact, just the reverse occurred. U. S. corporations and individuals, believing that an 8 percent devaluation was not the last word on dollar parities, and lacking confidence in the U.S. economy, left their money abroad. For all analysts this fact contained the seeds of a new and sustained crisis. The threat of a new monetary crisis continued to hang like a pall over any change in the direction of the U.S. economy, especially when in February and March dollars began their new flow toward Europe, forcing the nervous central banks once more to absorb immense new amounts to support the floor of the dollar rate. The price of gold rose to $50 on the free market, then to $70 by August, beginning its upward climb that would exceed $150 by 1974.

And in Europe, by mid-January 1972 the worst expectations were materializing. "It's quite clear now that Germany is in real stagnation. I don't see where any recovery is coming from, for the moment," reported the director of the Dresdner bank.[17]  Italian industrial production declined by 3 percent in 1971, the worst drop since World War II. In Benelux, investment was expected to fall 4-5 percent.

Washington, contrary to the prescriptions of economic orthodoxy but pursuing political exigencies, continued to follow its "Keynesian" program in a desperate, near hysterical effort to reduce unemployment and renew business confidence in a sagging economy before the November election. In January 1972 Nixon told the nation that "deficit spending, at this time, like temporary . . . controls, is strong but necessary medicine," and he proposed a fiscal 1973 budget deficit of $25.5 billion. The Federal Reserve intended "to price money so cheaply that corporate borrowers will simply be unable to resist it."[18]  The money supply grew by 12.7 percent in the first quarter and 11 percent in the second, and interest rates were lowered to 4 3/8 percent by March. Despite the statistical juggling, the Western European capitalists could only view this vast increase in American liabilities as further recklessness, and many in the U.S. worried about the long-term impact and the inflationary threat.

Regardless of all of Washington's efforts to generate expansion in the economy, unemployment was still forecast for 5.5 percent at the end of 1972. Government economists were adjusting to the fact that 5 percent must now be considered "full employment" in the U.S. because of "structural weaknesses" in the economy. A Treasury report concluded, "over the next few years the four percent unemployment rate as a national goal is not feasible without significant inflation." "More than 800,000 people" were "permanently deprived" of a job for structural reasons.[19]  Secretary Connally told a Congressional hearing, "I don't want to start another war just to get a few people employed."[20]  But he spoke too soon, for once more indicating the route toward renewed business revival, Nixon again escalated the violence — and spending — in Indochina.

### 1972 Escalation in Military Spending

As early as January 1972 the Nixon Administration, failing on every other front, made the decision to increase substantially military expenditures as an integral part of stimulating the economy for the election in November. This form of spending is traditionally the most palatable for a capitalist economy when the political preconditions demand, at least temporarily, speedy changes in the overall economy. As early as January, a 50 percent increase in the number of "air sorties" over Indochina was included as part of the comprehensive plans for increased expenditures. Government spending contributed $9.5 billion to renewed economic activity in the first quarter of 1972.

The spring offensive of the revolutionary forces in Vietnam was seized as an excuse to expand an effort that was already well underway. Nixon's escalation of the savage attacks, consuming vast resources in brutal destruction, in fact once again did fuel the American economy. Where before the increased expenditures would have brought an outcry from important elements in the ruling class, at this time there was little more than momentary concern over the possibility that Nixon may have jeopardized the highly coveted new relations with China and the Soviet Union through his "adventurous" mining of the North Vietnamese coast. Otherwise, the most savage escalation of violence in the war met with little objection, and the business indicators began to climb — to the relief of business circles.

More important, by far, in generating new confidence in the economy for all major sectors of the American capitalists was the new potential of trade with the U.S.S.R., a long standing aspiration that became a reality with Nixon's June 1972 trip to Moscow. With the promises of trade and investment potential in the billions over the next decade and beyond, the general business and specialized industrial press reflected the euphoria as they universally celebrated the end of the Cold War. For certain industries, such as Boeing, the China trade was also of immediate benefit, and the future

China market, a dream at the turn of the century, now appeared more than a mirage.

The pressure for trade and other relaxation of relations with the U.S.S.R. and China existed in the ruling class for some years. They did not become of overriding urgency, however, until the crisis in the U.S. economy and in world trade and investment had reached a critical stage in the summer of 1971. Nixon's announced visits to China and then to the U.S.S.R., while most dramatically focused on its effects on the Vietnam war, to American business was an economic step of the greatest significance. The rapid shift toward broad economic ties with the U.S.S.R., in particular, business viewed as Nixon's greatest achievement of his four years. The full dimensions of this new relationship for world capitalism I discuss in Chapter Six, but it is unquestionable that the renewal of business confidence in the second half of 1972 reflected the American industrialists' and bankers' assessment of their "new frontier."[21]

By April 1972, superficially it appeared that the Nixon Administration had restored, to a certain extent, some confidence among American businessmen as to the future of the American economy. The giveaway interest rates, the increased war expenditures, and the innumerable promises to all sectors, coupled with the profound caution on the part of the Europeans *vis-à-vis* the monetary situation, induced many corporations to increase their spending plans for capital goods despite the fact that U.S. industry was operating at only 75 percent capacity.

The administration put much weight on these signs of an upturn, but their artificial and inflated nature left the Europeans wary as to the future of the American economy, and the dollar remained a big question mark. They also suspected that much of the new flush was the result of a political manipulation for the 1972 election, and that after November the objective circumstances would force a sharp retrenchment.

In West Germany, all of the evidence of an impending recession motivated the Bonn government to introduce fiscal measures to try to stimulate the economy. Yet a deeper West German recession was circumvented chiefly because foreign orders, largely from the U.S., rose 14 percent during 1972. And by December 1972 the government was already again introducing anti-inflationary measures as consumer prices rose by 6.4 percent over the year.

The last half of 1972 continued to be a profitable period for American business. The government "pump-priming" had increased earnings enormously, Peterson was pressing forward on the Soviet markets, price and wage controls lent a note of stability, the low interest rates allowed for a rebuilding of liquidity and inventories, the dollar appeared stabilized, the protectionist interests had failed in their efforts with Congress, and peace was "at hand." General corporate profits had the biggest gain, rising some 15 percent over the year. But unemployment also remained high and plant utilization low.

The new year, by contrast, began badly. The massive bombing of the major cities of the DRV accentuated anti-American sensibilities which only hurt business interests, with no gains whatever. Nixon made several disagreeable shifts in personnel, replacing Peterson with Frederick Dent, representative of the protectionist textile industry. And there was stalling on several of the coveted Soviet trade agreements. And as expected, the Nixon Administration reverted to giving greater play to the "free market." Nixon's conversion to Keynesianism was expedient for 1972. Under the direction of the orthodox economist George Shultz, the Administration once more decided to cut radically federal spending, raise the interest rates, and drop the controls on wages and prices. So in January Nixon attempted to swing the economy into reverse. "We cannot keep inflation in check unless we keep Government spending in check . . . ," he announced as he introduced a deflationary budget and lifted controls on wages and prices.[22] Another "credit crunch" and recession were forecast and many economists anticipated a repetition of 1969-70. But in fact, the economic situation had not remained static over the intervening years. The entire world economy had changed structurally

*vis-a-vis* banks and credit, currency crises, and a collapse of
confidence. The entire system is so fragile that a new recessionary plunge carries with it much greater dangers for the
capitalist system.

While there were deafening testimonies on the good
health of the economy, those in control of vast funds showed
their doubts during the first week of February 1973 by again
rushing to exchange the dollar for other currencies. Within
days, as $6 billion once again poured into Germany, another
major dollar crisis led to a new devaluation of 10 percent and
a float of a number of key world currencies on February 12.
Last-minute fears of impending monetary chaos led the Western European political leaders to unite on a proposal that,
in essence, met the longstanding American demand for a
floating bloc of European currencies against the dollar. The
economies of England and Italy, all agreed, were too weak to
withstand a fixed parity against the stronger mark and franc.
The EEC's first "concerted initiative" was the one the U.S.
had long desired.

## The "Business Cycle"

With the integration of world capitalism, national economic policies are increasingly coordinated in their response
to crisis. And the key to the capitalist industrial economies
is still the fate of its largest member. The U.S. economy,
from the export of inflation to the recession of 1969-71, to
the intense monetary and fiscal stimulation of 1972 to the
retrenchment in 1973, has had rapid repercussions on the
economies of Europe and Japan. Over the past decades,
however, there was some lag between the business cycles of
various states and, as the Citibank newsletter noted in December 1971, "marching out of economic step is a virtue."[23]
Perhaps most significant of all, therefore, is that by mid-1973
this lag between the business cycles of the industrial states
had virtually disappeared for the first time since World War II.
In the past the cycles were staggered, and while a recession
in one country would often lead to a recession in the others,

the "recovery" in the first, likewise, would pull the others out. But in April 1973 *Business Week* quoted a U.S. Treasury official who, while discussing the fact that the business cycle of the industrial states now appeared to be synchronized, noted that "There is a danger that if all the big economic powers move up together, the day will come when they all move down together as various countries move to tighten their credit facilities to curb their booms."[24]

The Europeans hoped that a slackening in U.S. demand would help to curb their inflation (ignoring the consequent scramble for markets that would ensue with a general fall in demand), but they also began to take their own predictable steps to "slowdown" their own economies. These moves came less than two years after they were bemoaning an approaching depression. Nearly simultaneously, in mid-1973 the major industrial states raised their interest rates and began to reduce government spending. Following the major curtailments in U.S. government domestic spending in the 1974 budget, the French and German governments announced in May 1973 that they would apply "brakes" on public demand, and the Japanese government later in the month made it known that it also planned sharp cutbacks in government spending and new curbs on capital investment. During this period the British and Benelux governments also announced curbs on spending.

In the U.S. the prime interest rates of the commercial banks and the discount rate of the Federal Reserve reached historic peaks. *Le Monde* wrote on July 30 of a "war" of interest rates, as each member of the EEC was engaged in defending its own economy without worrying about the consequences for its "partners." As Germany applied deflationary measures with its interest rates, Britain was forced to raise its own to a record level to stop the outflow of currency. The upward pressure of the mark was also dragging up the other currencies pegged to it and making their products less competitive relative to the dollar. This led the Belgian Finance Minister to note, "Should the business cycle take a turn, it is plain that a definitely undervalued dollar would become unbearable for Europeans. They would be compelled to take serious measures to defend employment."[25]   In light of this fact they cannot help but move to protect their own interests at each level — from individuals through corporations through governments.

Inevitably, the industrial capitalist states reacted to the inflationary trends that followed so closely upon the recession with new restrictionist deflationary moves *vis-à-vis* interest rates, money supply, and government spending. One unanticipated effect of the 1973 devaluation in the U.S. was the greatly increased world demand for American food, raw materials, and industrial supplies which created shortages and further inflationary pressures within the U.S. Germany, France, Japan, Britain, Italy, and the U.S. were all following the same course by mid-1973. What with all the other unstable factors operating currently in the world economy, this new coordination of the business cycle is highly significant. These moves are unable to curb the worldwide, raging inflation because prices are beyond their indirect controls. Their measures can only heighten social tension.

By the end of 1973 the fourfold rise in oil prices accelerated these pressures. Government economists throughout Europe and Japan issued dire warnings of the impending worst recession since the Second World War or even a depression, coupled with seemingly uncontrollable inflation. The EEC officially predicted 5 percent unemployment in Europe. Many Japanese in government and industry, more pessimistic yet, foresaw little short of disaster for their economy in 1974. These governments began to take steps to avoid the worst consequences of the situation. Both the French and the Japanese permitted their currencies to fall sharply in relation to others and the spectre of competitive devaluations to win trade advantages was clear to all. In January 1974, France announced a 3- to 20-year barter deal with Saudi Arabia, trading weapons and technology for assured oil supplies and Britain shortly concluded a similar deal with Iran; Italy and Japan followed with overtures to Saudi Arabia. Fearing massive unemployment in oil-related industries

— one out of every ten workers in the EEC is in the auto or
its satellite industries — northern Europe terminated its recruitment of foreign workers and began to send many home,
thereby compounding the problems in the poorer countries.
The implications and contradictions of these moves were
clear to the governments concerned, but as with private
capitalists in general, the fact that the government leaders
"know" the dangers of trade war and competitive devaluations does not prevent their following such a course. Circumstances require that they respond to immediate domestic
needs. The manipulation of the American economy in 1972
was successful in transforming a recession into an apparent
world economic boom. The unprecedented deficits, giveaway credit, escalation of the war in Vietnam, and the monumental grain sales to the Soviet Union all played their part in
the cynical ambitions of Nixon for reelection. Already pro-
grammed in 1972 was the postelection retrenchment of the
supercharged economy.

But it may be considerably more difficult, short of
another war, to pull out of the next down-turn. The syn-
chronization of the business cycles among the industrial
countries is now very consequential. At the same time,
the credit structure is yet more vulnerable following the
period of overconfidence expressed in the latest period of
intense expansion. A collapse of a large bank or corporation
could trigger a chain reaction more far-reaching than those of
the last recession in the U.S. The struggle for markets likely
to ensue as all the industrial states "move down together"
will only intensify the political struggle among the governments concerned as each moves to protect its most powerful
sector and to try to minimize the political impact of economic crisis.

### CHAPTER TWO

## THE MULTINATIONALS: THE INTERNATIONAL
## CONCENTRATION OF CAPITAL AND ITS
## IMPLICATIONS

The phenomenon of corporations operating beyond their national borders is as old as capitalism itself. But there are, indeed, some crucial new dimensions in the present situation that have attracted so much popular attention to the so-called multinational corporations. During the nineteenth century, the investment banker played the leading role in the export of capital, which largely consisted of money-lending or portfolio investment operations without management control, save in colonies under direct political domination. There were, of course, exceptions. A few American companies even then preferred control via direct investment, particularly in petroleum and insurance. Direct U.S. investment overseas began on a large scale in the early twentieth century, mainly in raw materials and commodities but also partially in manufacturing. Yet prior to World War II only one to two hundred corporations were involved, and for most of these companies foreign operations were only a small part of their total activity. In this chapter, direct investment is the only really significant factor, for portfolio investment in foreign securities is a money market activity and differs little from deposits in a foreign bank to collect interest.

Until 1958 the most profitable area for American investment, with the exception of raw materials exploitation, was still in the U.S. itself chiefly because profits from Europe, where there was actually a higher rate, could not be repatriated. Then the confidence-shaking recession of 1957, plus the 1958 convertibility of the European currencies, gave the initial impetus to the vastly accelerated outflow of direct investment capital for the growing and profitable market in Europe. And the rising costs during the 1960s, plus the growing strength of foreign competition, initially stimulated the search among the American labor-intensive industries for reduced costs in the low-wage areas of the Third World. Thereafter and until this day, higher profit margins quickly became the sustaining drive for ever greater overseas expansion.

By 1965 there were 3,300 American multinational corporations controlling approximately 23,000 subsidiaries around the world, and the larger the corporation the more important were their overseas interests to their total profit and sales. Although this number has grown rapidly since 1964, more importantly in 1972 only 187 held three-fourths the total assets of U.S. investment abroad. At the same time there was a sharp acceleration in the concentration of capital in the U.S. itself. Between 1950 and 1968 the top 200 corporations' control of all manufacturing assets increased from 46 to 66 percent. It is these same 200 that control the preponderant sector of the overseas investment. Of the 1969 net earnings of all U.S. industrial corporations, the share of the top 87 was 50 percent or equal to that shared by the remaining 194,000 U.S. corporations. Of these top 87 corporations, only three do not have major overseas interests. And all the figures on assets and profits, according to the FTC report of 1969, were "greatly understated" — many corporations did not include their full foreign holdings.[1]

While there are increasingly multinational corporations from other capitalist states, the vast majority of the largest and most powerful are American, controlling 60 percent of all direct foreign investment in the world by the mid-1960s. For this reason, the very term "multinational corporation" is an ideologically burdened misnomer. These are primarily

American corporations exploiting multinational workers, using multinational capital, selling to multinational markets, and reaping multinational profits.

Far from being the paragon of efficient management or advanced technology, as its propagandists allege, and many others apparently believe, the basis of American corporate predominance rests on the U.S. government's political hegemony, America's vast internal resources exploited with unprecedented waste, two European wars which devastated its competitors even as they enriched America, two subsequent wars against Third World countries which further stimulated American economic growth through immense government expenditures, and, finally, the unique role of its national currency. The American corporations could not have achieved their dominant position in the world without this utilitarian oddity in global monetary arrangements. And it is astonishing to survey the volumes of tortured analyses that seek other factors, from "know-how" to superior management skills, for explanations.

But what is the significance in the fact that most of the giant multinational corporations are American? They do not act together as a league, nor is there more affinity between the subsidiaries of ITT and Ford than with any other European corporation. There is as much competition between Ford and GM abroad as between Ford and Fiat. "We don't consider ourselves basically an American company," asserted the vice-president of Ford Motor in charge of overseas operations. "And when we approach a government that doesn't like the U.S., we always say, 'Who do you like? Britain? Germany? We carry a lot of flags.' "[2] But the fact is that they are wholly American companies by any criterion. A survey of 1,029 chief executives of the largest U.S. multinational companies revealed that only 19 were not American citizens. And the foreign ownership in these same companies amounts to only about 3 percent of the common stock. Only the workers and nonequity capital are foreign.

The carefully cultivated myth of the multinational operating without national allegiance is deceptive in other critical regards. While it is true that the multinational corporation really carries only the flag of profit, and has no allegiance to national aggrandizement of aggregate U.S. interests, the fact that most of them are based in the U.S. and are, indeed, the most politically powerful corporations there, with usually the decisive voice in the formation of foreign policy where it affects their interests, means that Washington's policy will usually speak for them. While for the worker there is no difference in working for Ford or Fiat, obviously there is indeed a difference when a small nation engages in a conflict with the Philips Corporation leading to a confrontation with the Dutch government, and crossing the interests of General Electric or ITT and facing the American government.

But such questions as the so-called "national integrity and independence," the "unfair competition," the "loss of sovereignty in economic policy," and all the other expressions of rival capitalists that now fill reams of pages of criticism in the fashionable debate over the multinationals, are of no interest in this study. Rather it is critical to focus on what implications, if any, this concentration of capital on a world scale, politically supported by the world's most powerful nation, has for the future viability of the very capitalist system itself.

## The Extent of Concentration

The mere size and concentration of resources and capital in these vast new conglomerates injects a qualitatively new dimension into world capitalism. In 1946 the book value of U.S. direct investment was $7 billion, with one-half this sum in Latin America. The direct investment of American corporations abroad more than doubled between 1960 and 1970, from a book value of $32 billion to $78 billion. During the crisis year of 1971, not surprisingly, U.S. foreign investment soared to record highs, increasing $7.8 billion to a total of nearly $86 billion by 1972 and over $90 billion in 1973. The market value of this investment, of course, is much higher, and in 1972 it was estimated at $203 billion

— $78 billion in manufacturing, and $44 billion in petroleum. Most of the rise in new investment, or $5.2 billion, was in the industrialized countries. In the Third World new investment amounted to only $2.6 billion, chiefly in petroleum. The sales of the foreign subsidiaries of the top 200 corporations between 1960 and 1970 rose from $24 to $77 billion, and in 1972 exceeded $90 billion. Yet the oft-cited sales figures of many corporations which dwarf the GNP of many nations are of less significance for calculating their role in the world economy than the data on the financial transfers and transactions in which they engage, figures much more difficult to acquire. These vast flows of funds around the world are a critical attribute of the multinational firms. And while the parent corporation allows considerable autonomy to local managers over day-to-day production decisions, labor relations, and the like, it centralizes all financial dealings in the corporate headquarters, a trend that accelerated through the 1960s.[3]

The obvious basic motivation behind the rush of investment abroad, of course, is the higher rate of profit obtained increasingly from their overseas operations. A study of 178 large companies in 11 industries in July 1972 revealed that 122 received a higher rate of profit overseas than from their U.S. business. This fact only confirmed a consistent trend since 1964, when only 38 percent of the same group earned more abroad. The most important shift in this pattern occurred during the U.S. recession of 1969-70, when the percentage jumped from 47 percent in 1969 to 69 percent in 1971. Furthermore, in absolute terms, 90 corporations of the sample earned at least 25 percent of their total profits abroad, and 38 earned 50 percent or more. Among those firms earning more than half their total profits overseas in 1972 were such giants as IBM, UniRoyal, Honeywell, Woolworth, Coca Cola, Upjohn, Mobil, Pfizer, Gillette, Reynolds Metal, and Standard Oil (New Jersey). General Motors, the world's largest corporation, in 1970 earned 19 percent of its net earnings overseas, while Ford amassed 24 percent. While 1970 was an exceptional year for the auto industry

due to a strike in the U.S., it indicates the critical role played
by foreign investment to compensate even for such "difficult"
years. Moreover, the earnings of the foreign affiliates of
American firms in 1970 contributed 20 to 25 percent of the
total of *all* U.S. corporate profits after taxes. Despite the
accelerated economic activity in the U.S. during 1972, the
pattern of greater earnings in foreign affiliates continued.
Among the largest 200 industrials in the U.S. nearly all had
spectacular profit gains abroad in 1972 over the previous
year; Polaroid rose 30 percent, International Harvester
doubled its earnings, ITT received 45 percent of its net
earnings abroad, Procter and Gamble doubled in three years,
and all three auto companies reported exceptional gains.
The estimate of these same companies was that 1973 was an
even better year in terms of their overseas profits.[4]

### Incentives for Foreign Investment

Within the overriding framework of the pursuit of ever
greater profits, there are several distinct incentives for foreign investment, particularly in regions with protected markets, low wages, raw materials, subsidies of one sort or
another, or a combination of all these factors. Corporations
have no "master plan" for foreign investment decisions. This
could be assumed *a priori* from an understanding of how
capitalism operates, and surveys of leading corporations
confirm that each investment move is "made on its own
merits."[5] "The key factor of course is profitability," *Business Week* emphasized after a survey of the investment plans
of major corporations.[6] The motivations vary with specific
industries as well. Nearly all the large manufacturing corporations have subsidiaries in Europe for manufacturing and
marketing in order to secure access to the highly profitable
EEC market. By 1970 the EEC exceeded Canada for U.S.
investment, and in plans for future spending was scheduled
to move far ahead. The generous subsidies offered by the
different Western European governments have also attracted
them.

New investment, from whatever source, initially appeared to contribute to local prosperity, and Western European governments actually vied with one another to offer inducements to corporations to invest in certain underdeveloped regions or in industries that a government wished to see expand. These concessions gave the American corporations many advantages over their local competitors. The multinational corporations can and do play off competing governments, extracting advantages that leave the "host" country no benefit other than the employment provided. Tax provisions are either negotiated in advance, as with Belgium, or more commonly are of little importance as the corporations can transfer profits to their subsidiaries in countries with low taxes through intercompany loans, artificial consultation fees, interest payments, licensing, transfer prices, and the like. A 1970 EEC report on U.S. firms in Europe noted the irony of the European governments' competing to subsidize — offering as much as 30-40 percent capital grants for new plant construction — the richest corporations in the world, some with sales larger than their own GNPs. But the practice still continues. Ireland in 1973 was offering cash grants of 50 percent for construction costs and 15 years tax exemption. Such subsidies were doubly attractive when Ireland joined the EEC in January 1973. One-third of all American investment in West Germany is concentrated in the Hamburg area because of the "generous" investment environment, including 100 percent financing, tax advantages, subsidized land transport, port facilities built to order by the city, and the like.[7]

Under these conditions it is hardly surprising that the American corporations have an ever greater impact on the economic policies of the European governments. In Great Britain, U.S. firms by 1970 accounted for 14 percent of total output of British factories, 25 percent of its exports, and had 20 percent of fixed capital formation. In Western Europe, U.S. firms control 30 percent of the auto industry, 80 percent of the calculators and computers and more than 90 percent of the microcircuits. In West Germany, two

American oil companies control 50 percent of the market, and two of the top four auto companies are American — with GM's Opel leading in sales in 1972. U.S. investment throughout Western Europe has concentrated in the growth industries of the past 15 years — autos, oil, chemicals, metal working, as well as consumer industries — and not, as is often claimed, in those with the highest tariffs.

Again this investment pattern is of significance not in the sense of American corporations overwhelming Western European capitalists or challenging national sovereignty, but rather because the consequences of this concentration of capital, the centralization of decision-making, and the further *de facto* integration of the world economy leaves the national economies yet more swiftly vulnerable to a crisis that might begin in another part of the world. Hence it contributes to the destabilization of the capitalist economy on a world scale. For the decisions on whether or not to close or expand a production facility for an international corporation will of necessity be altogether different than that of a locally based capitalist who has no other options available.

The American corporation also often plays a role in applying political pressure on the governments of the industrial states on specific noneconomic policy issues. In particular, in France the American government was able to prevent the sale by French companies of goods to China or the Soviet bloc if they included parts made by a U.S.-owned firm. This extended even to a gift from General DeGaulle to Mao Tse Tung of several Caravelle planes because they included components made by American-controlled companies in France. More recently, in October 1972, the Pentagon and State Department, citing "security" reasons, vetoed a proposed joint venture between General Electric and the French aircraft corporation, SNECMA. Most observers understood the veto was for commercial reasons, and the furious French government sought means of retaliation through EEC tariffs. Finally, in June 1973, at the Nixon-Pompidou meeting, the issue was resolved in what was apparently a package deal on many political and economic issues, and Nixon approved GE's participation in the project.[8]

## The Banks

American banks have increasingly been attracted to
Europe and have begun to play a dominant role in finance,
especially with the expansion of the Eurodollar market and
the virtual absence of all restrictions on their activities.  The
financing needs of the giant multinationals and the international currencies' fluctuations have contributed to making
European activity the most profitable for many banks.  "In
our wildest dreams, we didn't think it would turn out as well
as it has," reported a vice-president of First National City
Bank of New York, which in 1971 earned 42 percent of its
net earnings from its overseas operations.[9]  The average return for the seven largest American banks was 28 percent of
their total profits.  Their foreign growth rate, on the other
hand, far exceeded that in the U.S.  In their new unregulated
theater of activity the banks have expanded into many new
channels impossible at home.  For instance, First National
City, along with its high-risk financing operations, now runs
a 100 percent owned cargo airline in Hong Kong and owns
75 percent of a Panama warehouse firm, among its total of
86 nonbanking subsidiaries in 20 countries.  More of their
activity is discussed in Chapter Three, but suffice it to say
here that the lure of high profits has induced the large banks
to take risks that could undermine the entire system, especially since it has steadily attracted new competition.[10]

It must be reiterated that now most of the expansion
of American firms involves no transfers of major value from
U.S. sources.  The American corporation plays only a type
of broker's role in their own financing.  The justifications
flowing from the multinational corporation's propaganda no
longer allude to the export of capital but to the contribution
of "know-how" and "advanced management," and that they
further integrate the world market.  First, they take advantage of the special privileges or the subsidy, then the financing
through borrowed European capital or the Eurodollar —
increasingly supplied by the Third World.  Both capital
markets are largely monopolized by these huge firms.  Finally,
there remained the exchange of overvalued dollars, although

the latter plays a lesser role. This foreign financing of
American expansion intensified after President Johnson
introduced mandatory curbs on capital export in 1968. In
1970 alone U.S. corporations borrowed a record $3 billion
abroad to finance their foreign investment of $6.8 billion,
bringing U.S. corporate foreign indebtedness to $11.3 billion
by the end of 1970. Recently there has been an increase in
floating Eurobonds to obtain new financing. The share of
European capital in America's foreign investment rose from
29 percent in 1959 to 47 percent in 1967, while the percentage of reinvested profits fell over the same period from
16 percent to 9 percent — although in 1972 there was a shift
in this trend as reinvested earnings doubled over 1971 from
$2 to $4 billion. As an EEC report on foreign investment
pointed out, after two to three years U.S. corporations need
no further dollars from home, and gave as an example General Motors, which over the past 20 years has not invested
one dollar in its enormous foreign investments.[11]

## Third World and the Multinationals

Although a survey of executives in the top 500 corporations revealed that seven to one preferred investing in the
industrialized nations, the highest rates of profit still are to
be found in the Third World. With investment a little more
than one-half the industrial world, the overall earnings were
slightly higher in absolute terms. The means of achieving
these high profits, despite the risks, is the higher degree of
exploitation of low-wage labor in both raw materials and
manufacturing. It is, of course, their very underdevelopment
that makes them enticing, and their economic development
would be, in many ways, inimical to the interests of the multinational corporations. Although there are many small capitalists who are attracted by the low wages in Mexico or the
Caribbean, of chief interest here are the giants who have far-
flung operations in both the industrial and Third World nations. Yet increasingly even the small undertakings are under
the umbrella of one of the large conglomerates.

The inducements of low wages as well as innumerable fringe benefits or subsidies for the corporate giants are most common in the Third World, with its parade of neo-colonial, corrupt, and subservient dictatorships that guarantee a period of "labor peace," generally long enough to reap a quick, handsome profit. And although basic confidence in long-term stability is distinctly absent, the promise of immediate gains is decisive. Oil companies' investments in 1971, for example, were about equally divided between production in the Third World and their European marketing and refining facilities. The consumer electronic industry has nearly abandoned the U.S. to set up production facilities in these low-wage regions of the world, chiefly South Korea, Taiwan, and Hong Kong, or has licensed Japanese firms to construct components or finished products for export to the American firms in the U.S. The imports of these products into the U.S. during the first nine months of 1972 increased 45 percent over the previous year, "reflecting buoyant demand here and the continued shift of production to foreign subsidiaries . . .," according to a Commerce Department report.[12] The magnitude of the profit differential in this policy was outlined by the president of Zenith Corporation, which in the fall of 1970 became the last radio corporation to move completely overseas. For a TV built in the U.S. the labor cost was $56; built in their new plant in Taiwan the equivalent cost was $4.50, nearly 12 times less. These industries are even now fleeing Taiwan in search of even cheaper workers elsewhere in Asia. Other labor-intensive industries are moving into Latin America, the Caribbean, and Mexico as their favored area of investment, with wages there ranging from 10 to 30 cents an hour. The impetus behind the drive for lower costs is to maintain ever higher profit margins, for the wholesale price is never lowered to meet competition. Even foreign investment in raw materials is also motivated by a drive for lower costs as much as by the need to secure materials in short supply in the U.S.[13]

### Threats to Property

In November 1971 the State Department sponsored a private meeting to discuss its role in questions of nationalization of American interests. Participating were representatives of the oil, copper, steel, and other industries likely to be affected. The unanimous view was that the question "is not whether these industries will be nationalized but when, and on what terms?"[14]  While theoretically these men may recognize the seizure of their mineral properties in the Third World as "inevitable," they never resign themselves to the fact when it pertains directly to their own interests. The examples of this lapse of sophistication are as frequent as the challenges to their property, and are discussed more fully in Chapter Five.

In many cases the multinational corporations have tried to circumvent this confrontation by establishing "joint ventures" with the "host" governments. This procedure is generally their last resort, since it limits their ability to coordinate with their other worldwide activity, which generally means manipulating prices, production, and profit. Nevertheless, the corporations are now giving intensive consideration to the problems of control without equity ownership in the Soviet bloc and probably will eventually try to apply such arrangements in the Third World if forced to it. There has been a plethora of conferences and consultations recently to ". . . pacify the populist feelings which are so vivid around the world against multinational corporations," to quote the United Nations' Undersecretary for Economic Affairs.[15]  But the consensus is that the task is impossible and that an era of conflict will define the future.


### Investment Insurance

The major U.S. corporations have never taken much interest in the government's investment insurance programs such as now exist in the Overseas Private Investment Corporation (OPIC). At the end of World War II there was some discussion of similar insurance schemes and the industrialists, aware that their interests far exceeded their actual or book investment costs, discouraged such efforts and pressed instead for bilateral investment guarantee treaties with foreign governments. But what they have always desired most are political guarantees by the U.S. government. The threat of expropriation is not over the rather piddling sums of initial investment, the loss of which is readily taken off taxes or is initially small due to multiple subsidies. The major threat is to the profits from future operations. ITT found no solace in its OPIC insurance coverage in Chile, and eventually was unable to collect it, nor did the U.S. copper industry — claims which in any case nearly wiped out OPIC and became mired in legal disputes.

Their belief that such small compensation would reduce political pressure in Congress or the Administration to act on their behalf has always been one of the chief reasons American industry has never shown much enthusiasm for the program. In any case, most of the regimes throughout the Third World are so busy vying with one another to offer bigger and better subsidies to the giant corporations that there is often barely any initial investment cost and almost immediate profit. As for petroleum, the expenses for exploration are great and the insurance does not and cannot cover a significant proportion of them. OPIC is of no consequence in the oil companies' calculations of investment and profits ranging in the billions of dollars.

OPIC's reserves and cash in April 1973 were $162 million, before any claims were paid for the copper nationalizations in Chile. And for those claims there were legal disputes between the companies and OPIC as to the amount covered; but even so OPIC acknowledged a total claim of $218 million by only three companies. In April 1973 the president of OPIC was trying to secure another $72.5 million from Congress. The agency denied ITT's Chilean claim, sending that dispute to arbitration in the courts. The irrelevance of this quixotic Congressional gesture to "insure" U.S. corporations is readily apparent. Industry wants more from the U.S.

government than insurance, and usually gets it in the end.
C. Gordon Murphy, president of Cerro Corporation, the
mining company whose copper mines were nationalized in
Chile, asserted, "American companies cannot be expected to
take the entrepreneur's risk without the entrepreneur's re-
ward. There is no international law that will let us operate
in this area, and therefore there must be cooperation in the
future between industry and government."[16]

### Trade and the Multinationals

The traditional division in the American ruling class
throughout American history has reflected the divergent
interests of the tariff vs. trade-oriented industries. Frequently,
as with the agricultural interests, both positions are pressed
simultaneously by the same industry. More simply, any firm
that suffers from even moderate competition can and does
seek tariff protection from Congress on an item-by-item or
industry-by-industry basis. And all corporations that earn a
significant share of their profits through trade or have foreign
interests struggle against these protectionist initiatives. The
latter historically represents, at least since World War I, the
most important and powerful industries in the nation. But
the high tariff interests, primarily agriculture, textile, and
apparel, now recently allied with the trade unions, have considerable political weight in Congress.

Over the decades there have been sporadic attempts,
generally following the business cycle, to attain overall legislation of a protectionist nature or all-encompassing legislation
promoting the interests of "free trade." Since World War II,
despite numerous verbal declarations, any attempt to embody
either position into a rigid principle has been defeated — both
the International Trade Organization in the late 1940s and
protectionist trade bills of the Burke-Hartke variety. Policy
has generally been responsive to pressure on an individual
basis. There is no consistency to be found on this issue —
there are only interests. But they are often competitive and
conflicting, and the attempt to resolve them to the satisfaction of all has only led to greater conflict or crisis.

The multinationals have divergent and contradictory policies even within the same corporation. Ford Motor, for example, needs an economic environment conducive to the free flow of capital and goods for its far-flung activities, but it is now alarmed by the threat of Japanese imports in the American market and is strongly protectionist. It is impossible to generalize, except to say that each corporation will act politically to promote profit and avoid loss, often in contradictory ways at the same time.

At first the easiest solution for the political men of any state in trying to meet the contradictory demands of all domestic constituencies is to put the onus and burden on other nations. But unless one state has undisputed dominance in the world political and economic arena, it is impossible to impose its order on a system that is intrinsically in chaos. Hence any move to protect one interest will lead to retaliation by other states against other interests.

The question of American foreign trade is preeminently a question of the multinational corporations. For not only is corporate control becoming ever more concentrated on a world scale but trade between states reflects this concentration. Only 298 multinational companies accounted for fully 51 percent of all U.S. manufactured exports and they imported 34 percent of total imports in 1970. And increasingly trade is a matter of transfers between the parent corporation and its subsidiaries. Total imports of parts and components, principally by parent companies from their subsidiaries, jumped from $850 million in 1965 to $3,300 million in 1969. Sixty percent of that total was from Canada. The Commerce Department estimated in 1970 that 25 percent of American manufactured exports reflected this intracorporate trade. Those industries locating overseas to take advantage of low-wage workers, particularly the electronic industries whose exodus was after 1970 and those industrial companies that expand abroad to avoid anti-pollution regulations, will all import from their own subsidiaries. In raw materials the proportion of intracorporate trade is even larger, as it is with most tropical food imports. With the increased foreign oil quotas the import of American-owned petroleum leaped 42 percent in 1972, and will continue to expand greatly in the future.

The international struggle for cheap labor and markets will only accelerate. What has happened in the electronic industry will occur in other industries as well. These corporations produce offshore not only for American demand but also aim at the Japanese and European markets. Other corporations from all over the world will do the same or erect further trade barriers. The U.S. will not act against the interests of its own largest corporations who are importing from their own subsidiaries. Significantly, the Administration's new trade bill excludes import restrictions from the "developing countries," supposedly to aid their economic advancement but in reality because they are U.S.-owned imports. U.S. affiliates in Europe, on the other hand, do not export to the U.S.

Renewed domestic protectionist pressure against the multinationals' worldwide activity mounted with the recession in 1969-70. As government orders fell, smaller domestic industries and the labor unions called for measures to curtail competitive imports and the export of jobs. The multinational corporations have organized propaganda efforts in the universities and press in response, purporting to prove that their role is beneficial to most of the problems in the U.S. economy as well as being the agent of progress and peace throughout the world. They decry nationalism as an archaic concept, and celebrate a functional division of labor. The Peterson Report of January 1972 was the most official and prestigious of these studies. A report of a committee from the Commerce, Treasury, Defense, and Labor departments, it anticipated a more active role on the part of the government in combatting the growing criticism of the corporate giants. Peter Flanigan, the President's assistant on international economic policy, elaborated to Congress a new thesis that perhaps the industrial worker in America was becoming an anachronism, and that just as the United States had moved from an agricultural to an industrial society it would now move from an industrial to a service society. As a less sanguine official put it, to a nation of "coupon clippers and welfare recipients."[17]  More explicitly, at the time the Administration viewed this corporate activity abroad as a major area of profitability and their income as the major positive figure in the balance-of-payments in the U. S. economy.  That the combination of these powerful multinational corporations in the U.S. would prevail should never have been in doubt. However, Nixon's erratic behavior had also generated fears and irritations for them.

### The Deficit in Trade

It is true, as some have suggested, that Presidents and Secretaries of State in general regard issues of trade and economic policy as dull and technical questions.  Unlike grand diplomacy and military strategy, they can be left to others, or dealt with in a piecemeal manner within the unvarying framework of the axiomatic assumptions of the system.  This is true until corporate affairs in some part of the globe provoke an individual political crisis, or the compilation of specific policies cumulatively provokes an overall crisis — whether trade, monetary, or systematic.  If nothing else, the trade statistics forced a political response to precisely such a situation in 1971, when there was no way to hide the fact of a trade deficit of $2.1 billion that was declared to be the first in the century.  And everyone recognized early in 1972 that, despite the monetary manipulations, the deficit would worsen sharply.  By the year's end there was a deficit of $6.8 billion, more than three times the record in 1971, but in reality it was even worse than generally believed.

The U.S. government has, indeed, manipulated its trade figures to hide the true balance of commercial trade that would give an accurate index of its position in the world market.  In 1971 there was some dispute within the Administration and with the protectionist interests in Congress over this fact.  The Commerce Department includes in its trade figures those exports financed by grants of the AID and P.L. 480 food programs and excludes from the import figures, unlike most nations of the world, the shipping and insurance costs to the American border. If the trade figures are made truly comparable to those of other nations, the U.S. has had a trade deficit every year since 1966, with a total cumulative deficit from 1966 through 1970 of $15 billion. In addition, the deficits of 1971 and 1972 would be that much greater. Both because it would strengthen the protectionist cause and create general alarm over the real state of the economy, George Shultz declared in 1970 that it would be "inadvisable" to present such figures "prominently . . . on a regular basis."[18]

By other criteria, the American share of world manufactured exports fell from 25 percent in 1960 to 19.6 percent in 1970, and this downward trend was accelerating into the 1970s. In West Germany, the major American market in Europe, the U.S. share of imports has shrunk to fourth place since 1965, when it was the chief supplier. And this eclipse is of interest to the same multinational corporations that dominate the foreign investment.

In mid-1972 leading Administration spokesmen were once again evaluating the general economic picture and reflecting on possible solutions. Reportedly the most recurrent themes were a formalization of a world system of blocs and greater government-business partnership to promote exports and more effectively speak for U.S. business abroad. When questioned about the need of America's largest corporations for additional subsidies, tax writeoffs, merger privileges, and diplomatic muscle in contract disputes with foreign governments, then Secretary of Treasury Connally retorted, "Hell . . . compare what we do for American business interests to what Japan does."[19]

In fact, the Administration released reports that it was studying the Japanese social system as perhaps being the key to Japan's immense success in the field of foreign trade, a reaction comparable to the Europeans, both East and West, assuming American success was linked to management "know-how." Perhaps more than any other capitalist nation, Japan has a total merger of its business and political elite. This wholly "board room" government was discussed in Washington as a model and a highly efficient means by which to meet the new crisis of America's role in the world economy. To compete in the new competitive arena of world trade, as well as to aid the expansion of American interests abroad, the U.S. would require a strengthened business-government partnership. It was a reflection of the mood and new responsiveness of the Nixon Administration-to the critical sector of American economic interests. Sweeping changes were needed in the American system to give its industry the competitive force it now lacked, "a transformation . . . is going to have to happen . . .," again to cite Secretary Connally.[20]

The Administration's fear that the U.S. could no longer compete in world trade had been under the closest study and the outlines of the new strategy began to emerge in the spring of 1972. Once more it took the form of the most powerful sector of U. S. capitalists defining their own interests for the state policy to follow. The irritation of certain multinational corporations, such as ITT, over Washington's weak response to nationalization threats to their interests elicited promises for greater government involvement. The giant corporations' annoyance with anti-trust legislation and restrictions on capital flow were assuaged by promises to eliminate these archaic restraints. The irritation over trade barriers in Europe once more received prime attention. Each concession to these interests, however, contains the seeds of new conflict and crisis. For as American negotiators with the EEC attack every specific trade barrier to U.S. exports as a life-and-death issue, men such as the former U.S. Ambassador to the EEC Robert Schaetzel, worry about the effect on U.S. investment: "U.S. businessmen in Europe are unhappily aware that powerful forces are ranging themselves against [them]. The 'Europe Firsters' will be strengthened by abrasive confrontations over the key issues of trade, agriculture and money."[21] The U.S. for its part, of course, has erected every form of protectionist device, from high tariffs, quotas, subsidies, tied loans, and dumping practices to "Buy American" provisions.

On the level of broad planning for the future of the

American economy in the world, certain hints were appearing from Washington that plans were underway for a new monetary and trade structure to be based on four economic blocs. Akin to the sterling bloc that was the anathema of U. S. policymakers at the end of World War II, such a system appeared a possible solution to America's endemic trade crisis. Each trade and currency bloc would maintain fixed parities, "free trade" and balance-of-payments within the bloc, and the blocs would float against each other and maintain a tariff structure similar to the EEC. The dollar bloc would include, according to the contemplated plan, Canada, Latin America, Japan, Indonesia, Australia, and the Philippines. There would also be a European bloc including most of Africa, the ruble bloc, and China. It was a crude concept and one that hardly reflected reality, for in practice the U.S. could not implement it. While it was anxious to alleviate its own problems in the aggregate, the U.S. government will continue to press its advantage wherever individual American interests are involved. The Japanese leaders were not of a mind to cooperate in such restrictions and are actively roaming the world in search of supplies and markets. None of these grand global schemes can be realized, and the best the Administration could achieve was an occasional bilateral diplomatic trade-off of a strictly transitional nature, as apparently occurred between Nixon and Pompidou in June 1973 relating to such questions as Africa and Southeast Asia, an accord in shreds by the year's end.

Given the difficulties at arriving at any overall solution, Washington is engaged in a feverish attempt to increase American exports. Nixon established a "Competitive Assessment Division" to evaluate such items as competitive labor costs, divergent pollution regulations, and anti-trust handicaps. And the State Department has told the U.S. ambassadors, especially in Europe, that their primary function is now to secure orders for American business. The State Department announced its campaign to promote American exports in June 1973, ironically the same day that Nixon put a boycott on the sale of soybeans, America's biggest export.

The Administration has concentrated most of its direct

attacks on the EEC, and Nixon declared 1973 to be the "Year of Europe," a direct acknowledgment of the impending crisis there in trade and monetary affairs. The reservoir of conflict and ill-feeling, discussed in Chapter Four, had risen to the point where many political leaders and businessmen spoke in terms of the certainty of economic war, and occasionally even expressed hopes that the conflict would not extend beyond economics. The *Wall Street Journal* on February 1, 1973, reported that "relations between the U.S. and Europe are widely agreed to be the worst since World War II. . . ." In fact, in trade the U.S. had a surplus with the Community, except for a slight deficit in 1972, since it was organized in 1958. In 1971 its major exports — grain and soybeans, aircraft, computers, and machine tools — rose by 10 percent despite the growing stagnation or recession in the European economies. But by the end of 1973, the "Year of Europe" proved to be no more than a slogan, as none of their points of conflict was resolved and were in fact exacerbated by the conflict in the Middle East. Yet in trade diplomacy the U.S. will continue its style of ultimatum and insult, lodge major protests on the most inconsequential issues of trade, and press with threats for a modification of the EEC tariff and so-called nontariff barriers to American exports. But this European target of the new U.S. trade offensive is a relatively minor factor in its trade deficit and the modification of these barriers would not significantly change the situation.

Applying all these pressures and counterpressures, and reacting to the trade and payments statistics with little reflection as to the causes, the American government intends aggressively to force other states to compensate for its endemic difficulties. It will try to get as much as it can for as many divergent corporate interests as possible. But the world has obviously changed over the past 25 years. Europe and Japan are strong, in great part as a side effect of the American policies of the past decades, and the governments there are responsive to identical pressures from their own capitalists. There is no possibility that the world capitalist powers will be able to make an agreement acceptable to all major interests. The Nixon Administration began in 1973 by preparing a trade bill that accused the other nations of "cheating" the U.S., threatening that they will not negotiate until the "cheating" stops, and after the dollar devaluation, trade spokesmen began to discuss a new surcharge on imports.[22]    The Europeans indicated that they were in no hurry to proceed with trade negotiations. So as each nation or bloc of nations acts, and reacts, to protect the competing interests of its own nationals, conflict and crisis will grow steadily more acute. The areas of conflict in trade are multiple, and they are far more fundamental than monetary crises which in large part only reflect the jockeying for trade advantage. In periods of economic expansion the conflict will be for raw materials and in periods of decline or recession there will be competitive struggle for markets. The two areas of trade that offer a possible safety valve for these pressures are the markets in the Soviet Union and China. But those markets, too, are bound to provoke the keenest competition between the varying capitalist interests.

There are many disgruntled powerful American interests that continue to respond negatively to Nixon's "tough" diplomacy, since any trade initiative touches directly the interests of the multinational corporations. Such sensitive organs of traditional foreign investment and trade-oriented opinion as the *New York Times* editorialized angrily over the risks of achieving short-run gains for special interests at the expense of a sharp deterioration of the general trade and investment environment. Forcing concessions on Japan and the European Community on quotas for textiles and steel, many interests feared, would only add to the grievances over which there was certain to be a future accounting, possibly threatening the investment climate or contributing to retaliatory measures against other important trade interests. Abrasive diplomatic encounters in the European Community, GATT, or IMF increase anxiety in general, but the ultimate test will be in the Western European and Japanese reaction. "Washington still ignores the cumulative effects of small actions on its larger interests," warned Robert Schaetzel, the former U.S. ambassador to the EEC. "We are drifting close to an irrevocable national commitment to a tough line. Before taking that step, we should consider the larger American interests at stake, and the probable high costs of diplomacy by confrontation."[23] Nevertheless, diplomacy must respond to the power realities of the times. An agreeable and diplomatic negotiating tone on the part of the Nixon Administration will no more alter the underlying economic conditions, which cannot be reconciled within the present economic context, than the "tough" stance.

### Conclusion

It is true that the massive concentration of industrial and financial power is a new dimension in world capitalism, one that allows the giant corporations a scope for action that can accelerate and aggravate economic crisis on a worldwide basis. The fact that production facilities are expendable in one part of the world and easily transferred to another creates a greater readiness to terminate production and arbitrarily transfer capital at the slightest increase in cost or any other unfavorable economic trend. The multinational corporations can hasten economic crisis on a world scale by their rapid overreaction to changes in the business cycle. They contribute to the acceleration of economic crisis in world capitalism and are themselves extremely vulnerable to it.

It is equally important, however, in understanding the multinationals' role in the world economy not to exaggerate or misunderstand their power. The competitive aspects of world capitalism intensify demonstrably with the trend toward the concentration of capital. The American government will respond to protect and advance the interests of those companies which represent the most politically powerful sector of American capitalism, but action which it takes to alleviate the problems of one corporation will aggravate the problems of another. One cannot define the collective interests of American corporations abroad as if they represented a monolith, for the struggle between them is too intense. The continual comparison by some of the GNPs of industrial states to the consolidated sales of the MNCs is a misleading and irrelevant point. Corporations are not nations, and the world is still very much in the stage of national capitalism. The industrial nations respond to diverse and competitive pressures, have different motivations for action, and have powers which exceed those of the larger corporations. In the Third World, however, these corporate giants generally play a different role and often are the sole political and economic power in small nations, such as in Central America and some countries in Africa.

Ultimately, the real significance of the multinational corporations is not only their immense concentration of wealth and power but their destabilizing role in the capitalist world economy. It is this catalytic function that poses the most immediate menace to capitalism today, threatening to expose and interact with all its other formidable structural weaknesses.

### CHAPTER THREE

## MONEY AND THE DOLLAR CRISIS

Hegemony, not liquidity, is what the dollar problem is all about," asserted a vice-president of First National City Bank (Citibank) to a Congressional committee in 1970.[1] This proposition is perhaps restating the obvious, for even the problem of liquidity — the dollar glut — rests on the unique postwar position of American currency in the world's economic relations. This hegemony of the dollar has reflected America's economic and political dominance and has been a primary instrument in expanding it. In turn, it has been both a barometer of, and contributor to, the developing crisis in world capitalist relations.

America's predominant, indeed exclusive, position of power and production at the end of World War II enabled it to establish the dollar as the world currency acceptable to all as a monetary reserve and standard of parity. With the 1944 Bretton Woods Agreement the Federal Reserve Bank became the *de facto* central bank for the entire capitalist world. The rest of the world's shortage of dollars, the so-called "dollar gap," at that time appeared impossible to bridge and Washington's attempt to do so to secure markets for American production led to sundry programs of grants and loans ranging from the Marshall Plan to "offshore procurement" for military assistance, support of occupation forces throughout Europe and Japan, grants-in-aid around the world, export subsidies, and the like. The Korean war, however, was the

53

critical factor in transforming the U.S.'s postwar balance-of-payments from surplus to deficit.

Between 1950 and 1957, when the dollar was considered "as good as gold," the world's central banks as well as private bodies felt it was even better than gold, for they could "buy" U.S. Treasury short-term securities and earn interest (which outweighed any risk of devaluation), or use the dollars in settling accounts with other nations, or even loan them in the private money markets at good interest. This confidence in the dollar remained strong over these years despite the fact that the U.S had a balance-of-payments deficit of an average of $1.6 billion annually between 1950 and 1956 because of massive government expenditures abroad. Until 1957 the U.S. was a net importer of short- and long-term private capital. This pattern was reversed in 1958, when foreign money was withdrawn from the American economy and $2 billion in gold returned to Europe. The exchange of foreign-owned dollars for U.S. Treasury bills in effect granted loans to the U.S. with which to finance its mounting overseas deficits each year. This reflected confidence in the strength of the American economy, which, buoyed by the expenditures for the Korean war and the continued expansive policy of its aftermath, superficially remained an area of profitable investment. As late as September 1957, the *Economist* could headline an article "The Dollar Gap Again" and express concern over low U.S. imports and the "tremendous demand abroad for American goods," particularly transportation equipment, chemicals, and electric machinery. During 1957 "hot money" sought a haven in the U.S.[2]

As noted in Chapters One and Two, these conditions altered radically over 1957-58 with the combination of a falling rate of profit in the U.S., a sudden deflationary policy which accelerated a sharp American recession, and the organization of the EEC with its free currency convertibility into dollars. Private U.S. investment dollars, which had earlier flowed largely to the Third World for raw materials, now virtually raced to the Common Market for investment in manufacturing. The small American payments surplus of

1957 was followed by a deficit in 1958 twice as large as any earlier year. The deficit of 1958 generated anxiety among some Washington officials who seemed to feel that the situation of U.S. financial dominance could change swiftly. "One of these days," Secretary of Treasury George Humphrey wrote to Joseph Dodge in September 1958, "somebody is going to decide that they would rather have their money at home than here, and if our annual deficits of the past continue into the future just 'hang onto your hat' when the wind starts to blow."[3]    Official dollar liabilities to foreigners first exceeded U.S. gold reserves in 1959. In 1960 it was obvious that confidence in the dollar was shaken as private interests for the first time since 1945 turned a half billion dollars into their central banks, which now demanded gold instead of Treasury bills for their year's dollar surplus. Experts recognized that the shift represented a potentially serious crisis in world economic relations but there was, naturally, wide disagreement as to cause and cure.

The rapidity of the shift is notable, and over the subsequent decade irreversible changes developed in the very structure of the world economy. Attempts to manipulate the American economy via changes in the interest rates or money supply between 1958-62 only hastened the dollar outflow. U.S. corporations borrowed at low interest at home to invest in Europe. Direct investment increased from an annual rate of $400 million in 1959 to $850 million in 1961. The overall output of U.S. plants in Europe increased 22 percent over the same years. The shift had a direct effect on American exports, which declined in the transportation and electrical machinery industries between 1957 and 1960, while overseas production of the same American-owned industries rose by 50 percent. The bulk of the new investment went to the EEC, and of that amount one-half flowed into Germany. The same period saw a reduction in new investment in the Third World, which was increasingly channeled into manufacturing instead of raw materials — all through the medium of the omnipotent dollar.

This new influx of dollars through private investment

led to boom conditions in Europe while the U.S. was still responding to a recession at home with lower interest rates. European governments began to blame the unrestrained dollar inflow for their own inflation and tried to raise interest rates to manipulate the economic environment in the traditional orthodox capitalist manner. The high rates merely increased the dollar inflow of short-term capital in quest of the higher interest. Many American corporations at this time moved large dollar cash reserves to Europe.

Due to these pressures on the balance-of-payments and the implications for the American economy in the future, the U.S. government began to take some faltering steps to alter the situation. In 1961 Washington made agreements with Germany to "offset" its huge expenditures for its occupation forces, whereby Germany would buy American military equipment. It also tied a greater proportion of its aid funds everywhere to purchases in the U.S. and reduced its offshore procurement program substantially. The government also introduced a few measures to control the export of capital in 1963 and 1964, steps that primarily affected the foreign lending of U.S. banks. The controls had little consequence other than to move the capital market in dollars from New York to Europe, primarily London. Direct lending abroad by American banks from their home office virtually ended in 1965, but they were prompted to open branches in Europe to be free of all U.S. restrictions and to profit from the growing demand for, and supply of, what came to be known as "Eurodollars." These measures altered slightly the outflow of dollars for investment in 1965, but the balance-of-payments worsened in such categories as trade for different political and economic reasons.

Prior to 1965, in brief, there was a major shift in the dollar's position in the world economy and a substantial outflow for foreign investment, all of which took advantage of the unique role of the dollar in the monetary system, but also reflected growing doubts as to the U.S. economy and its relatively inadequate rate of profit. And these developments undermined confidence in the dollar throughout the world on both a private and governmental level.  Finally, these trends, as everyone knows, were accelerated in geometric proportions in 1965 and thereafter by the massive escalation of the Vietnam war and the outright balance-of-payments deficit which deteriorated annually at an average of $1.2 billion between 1964 and 1968.

During 1965, according to an official U.S. report, "Demand pressed against . . . capacity . . . lengthened delivery times . . . and less aggressiveness by U.S. firms in selling in foreign markets . . .," all weakened the U.S. trade position.[4]  The growth in government war purchases increased production and reduced unemployment.  For the first time since 1957 the price index rose sharply; it had been relatively stable between 1957 and 1964, resting on the foundation of an unemployment rate that hovered between 5 and 7 percent.  Although the net payments outflow of military expenditures increased 90 percent due to the Vietnam war between 1965 and 1968, many economists recognize that the effects of the war in undermining the dollar, the balance-of-payments, and the American economy were not only by increased expenditures overseas, but through its powerful inflationary impact on the domestic economy — which I discussed in Chapter One.  Due to this heightened consciousness of the balance-of-payments position of the U.S., the government made considerable effort to confine spending for the war to the American economy.  In fiscal 1969 the Vietnam outlays were estimated to be $28.8 billion, $27 billion of which was spent in the U.S.  The direct balance-of-payments cost was considered $1.8 billion.  The indirect costs, however, were far higher.  Listed as private imports were, in fact, materials used for war production in the U.S.  The enlarged government demand on the U.S. industrial capacity increased prices, reducing the competitive edge of American goods.  The availability of government contracts and the war-induced boom in the home economy led to a loss of interest in exports and, finally, to a permanent loss of overseas markets.  The same "boom" increased the demand for imported consumer and industrial goods not produced by the U.S. industry preoccupied with war orders. To finance the unprecedented budget deficits the government massively increased the money supply, further undermining confidence in the American currency. And reflecting the simultaneous growth of U.S. corporations overseas, dollars became at once more abundant, weaker in terms of the general confidence in them, and more volatile.[5]

Politically the war was too unpopular to be financed through increased taxes, and the costs had to be met through deficits. This supposedly peripheral conflict in Indochina struck directly to the heart of the system. Although the economy boomed from 1965 to 1968, the foundation of the dollar, already shaken before the escalation of the war in 1965, crumbled with the deficits both in the budget and international payments. For while the American corporations were enriched individually, their economic environment and their currency were undermined. And these structural changes led in subsequent years to greater deficits and greater crises.

### The "Dollar Crisis"

Given this background of the progressive undermining of both the value of the dollar and confidence in its stability *vis-à-vis* gold and other currencies, all of which was based on a lack of confidence in the American economy and alarm over Washington's unprecedented "mismanagement" of economic policy, any hint of a worsening of the situation or any movement of other currencies will provoke a massive flight from the dollar. The system is not coordinated, and each one must watch out for himself — meaning corporations, banks, oil sheiks, and whoever is a holder of massive liquid funds.

At the slightest hint of any possible revaluation, the corporate money managers and bank currency traders alike move as an immense herd to hedge against loss or to make a profit. It is, of course, silly to envisage these men as plotting or gambling against the dollar as if their motives had political implications. Their role as money managers requires that they move swiftly and in force in strictly business operations, even though the cumulative consequence will be directly in conflict with their long-term interests. This "defensive" reaction, as executives call it, neither justifies nor condemns their individual acts. It is the very essence of the capitalist system that they must act in this manner. And it is simply one more sharpening contradiction in the structural framework of contemporary capitalism.

A recent U.S. Tariff Commission study of the link between massive speculative capital flow and the American corporate giants estimated that at the end of 1971, of the total $268 billion in the international money market (more than three times the total official world reserves), U.S. banks and corporations controlled $190 billion, or 71 percent. This merely indicates the concentration, since all capitalists, regardless of nationality, will act with the same motive. But it takes only a small fraction of these sums to force shifts in the parities of currencies. In the weeks prior to the 1973 devaluation, the American banks' net outflow of funds was $4.6 billion in contrast to $177 million during the same period in 1972. This does not take account of Eurodollar transfers into other currencies which were also massive. The profits, of course, are equally immense, and those transferring funds made at least $500 million on the dollar devaluation of February 1973 alone. In reality it is more the avoidance of loss since, except to repay the short-term dollar loans, there will be few reconversions back to dollars given the persistent lack of confidence in the currency's new parity. By the end of February 1973, as in the first months of 1972 following the first devaluation, everyone noted this failure to reconvert, as well as the immediate "realization" that the devaluation would have no impact on trade price advantage but merely result in higher profits for the exporters and higher prices in the U.S. The U.S. trade surplus in 1973 was less the result of devaluation than the world's shortage of food and industrial materials, coupled with temporary price controls that encouraged U.S. industry to seek higher prices abroad. These factors represented only a very temporary phenomenon.

These are not temporary currency flights, but are fundamental structural changes indicating the weakening base not merely of the dollar but of the American economy, along with its profitability and productivity. These questions are relative, of course, and can shift with changes in conditions of other economies. But by 1972 the U.S. was already for several years at the bottom of the list of the industrial nations for reinvestment of earnings and also held bottom rank for productivity per man hour — even lower than Britain. Most important, the larger profit margins for the major corporations were attributable to their foreign investments. Profits in the U.S. had steadily deteriorated with inflation during the 1960s. In 1972, by contrast, profits rose 15 percent and continued to climb into 1973, but there was uniform concensus that this was an extremely transitory situation and that the underlying condition of the American economy was weak.[6]

### The Eurodollar

Part of the fuel for stoking the periodic dollar "crises" comes from the well-known Eurodollar market. An only vaguely understood and increasingly feared source of highly volatile funds, there was an estimated $80 billion — or twice the amount of two years earlier — on deposit in Europe in February 1973, primarily in branches of U.S. banks. These figures fluctuate, and in any event, are highly questionable — for the reasons which follow.

Although allegedly started by the Russians in the early postwar years, the chief impetus for a significant European dollar market came with the expansion of American corporations in Europe in the early 1960s, especially after Washington's restrictions on capital flow and banking regulations between 1965 and 1968. Anyone — individuals, corporations, central banks, governments — can make deposits. When the Eurodollar interest rates are high, and they are always slightly higher than those in the U.S., dollars pour in from every corner of the globe, including from American foreign-aid recipients. Unlike U.S. banks until mid-1973, the Eurodollar deposits could collect interest for less than 30 days, and these deposits accounted for the large bulk of the transactions. Similarly, virtually anyone can borrow. In many cases this form of readily convertible liquidity allowed European corporations to borrow Eurodollars when domestic interest rates were too high as a result of their governments' adopting orthodox monetary means to curtail inflation. The corporations simply changed the dollars into domestic currency for further economic activity. The same procedure occurred during the credit "crunch" in the U.S. during 1969-70.

### The Double Count and Its Implications

International bankers and the business press have focused some attention on the "bewildering" question of double-counted Eurodollars, and the fact that in 1971 an estimated $13 to $25 billion being used in business transactions of all sorts does not exist at all.

Double counting was most common before May 1971, when the central banks were feeding the dollars they absorbed into the Eurodollar market through the Bank of International Settlements (BIS) in Basle. The process worked as in the following example: the German central bank receives a dollar from a local bank and loans it to the BIS for interest. The BIS in turn loans the dollar to a bank in London, from whom it is borrowed by a Dutch corporation. This corporation uses the dollar to import from a German company, which then exchanges it in the central bank where it is again listed as a new dollar — and the cycle begins once more, as the dollar becomes two or more in the economy. This is of consequence when the movement goes in reverse and repayment is required. Some economists have pointed out that "if there were no central bank as lender of last resort, there could be a financial collapse."[7] The process can

also operate without central bank deposits through the multiplicity of interbank dealings.   This ephemeral nature of paper
money based on the dollar is further compounded by the fact
that for each dollar exchanged by the central banks they are
required to print their own currency, and so with the multiplicity of dollars there is an additional multiplicity in other
currencies.  Added to the fact that the dollar has lost its
convertibility, has suffered two devaluations in 14 months,
and the U.S. Treasury has steadily undermined, from a conservative point of view, confidence in the dollar by pursuing
rampant inflationary policies even while incurring a spectacular debt both domestically and internationally, the role
of the Eurodollar is obviously cause for serious anxiety
among bankers.  But even though these billions of dollars
may be literally nonexistent, they are registered as claims
and as such have a dynamic role in the flow of money.  And
the confidence, or lack of it, which it generates is then transferred into the real world of economic and political activity.

Nevertheless, overriding in significance such questions
as double counts and even speculation, though they are all
intimately linked, are the recent developments in the credit
market for Eurodollars throughout the world.  The cumulative and current practices of the major banks dealing in
Eurocurrency can have the most profound impact on the
world capitalist system.

### The Eurodollar Market

The international financial markets today are a throw-
back to the old buccaneer days of unregulated enterprise and
"cut-throat competition."  It is an activity of unprecedentedly
high risk and high profit:  high profit for a few banks, and
high risks for the entire world capitalist system.  "There is no
security, no collateral, no mortgage, no specific guarantees,"
the vice-president of Citibank anxiously quoted *Barron's* on
the Eurodollar credit market.[8]  And for the banks there are
no regulations or reserve requirements whatever.  An incredible
house of cards has been constructed over the past few years

because of these enormous sums of dollars, often counted many times and placed on deposit in the banks of Europe. The transactions are in the hands not of traditional bankers but exchange traders, who with their huge stacks of Euro-dollars on short-term deposit — from overnight to six months — start looking for ways to make a profit. They are busy sending calls around the world to see who will take their money at marginal interest differentials. And as the margin of interest falls with increased competition, the volume of loans must be larger and therefore made to borrowers at ever-greater risk. As one study of the Eurodollar pointed out, banks carelessly lend $1 million at 1/16 of 1 percent margin and risk losing all for a three-months' profit of $181.25. Transactions of millions of dollars are made by telephone or telex in a matter of minutes, and for rarely less than $500,000. For the banks dealing in Eurocurrency loans the competition has grown intense and the transactions are in a kind of limbo where normal criteria of bank lending do not apply at all.

While initially in the hands of the largest American banks with branches in London, the lure of windfall profits has brought competition scurrying from every corner of the globe, and with them rising risks and a steady lowering of profit margins. In mid-1965 there were only 13 American banks with foreign operations via their 188 branches abroad, and their total foreign assets amounted to $7.5 billion. By March 1973 the figures had swollen incredibly. One hundred six American banks had foreign operations and 600 branches, and their total assets amounted to $92 billion — more than a twelvefold increase. By the end of 1972 there were 123 for-eign banks in London alone, 35 of which were American and doing the bulk of the business, with another 12 or so planning to open the following year. These include much smaller banks, such as North Carolina National and others, paying an average of $50 a square foot for office space and a mini-mum of $500,000 a year operating cost. The Bank of England, to reduce risks, decided in 1973 not to permit any more banks with less than $1 billion in assets to open branches. The British are reluctant to introduce other controls for fear all the Eurodollar business would move elsewhere. There is a belief among many depositors that the U.S. branch banks are safer, although the parent firms explicitly state that they do not guarantee the deposit.

The competition on the continent has grown enormously as well, with most of the major European banks being deeply involved. French banking, in particular, is heavily into international loans, which have grown from $2.5 billion in January 1967 to $14 billion in January 1972. The Swiss and Belgians were also greatly enlarging their activity by the end of 1972. Finally, the Japanese banks received government permission also to enter the fray. The Tokyo government, until the oil crisis in 1973, made its swollen dollar reserves — $18 billion in February 1973 — available to Japanese banks and they were being used not only to repay old debts but for lending in the Eurodollar market. The Japanese bankers became expert at "shaving margins" and in 1972 were able to "capture" loans to two giant American corporations — IBM and Chrysler. These same bankers were quoted as grateful for the spread of American "innovations" in introducing the novel "idea of making unsecured loans."[9] Recently even Singapore has developed as a center for an expanding "Asiadollar" market. By the end of 1972 the available funds exceeded $1.2 billion, three times the amount in 1970.

Moreover, not only banks are engaged in this great gamble but also such giant corporations as oil, tobacco, and others play the role of banks in the Eurodollar transactions and lend as well as borrow. Insurance companies invariably are only lenders. And, increasingly, funds are coming from the Third World, particularly the Middle East. As one authority on the subject put it, ". . . we have the phenomenon, of the lesser developed countries financing the developed ones."[10] "Starting this year," claimed the European director for the First Boston Bank in October 1972, "the Middle East will become an aggregate capital exporter."[11] These funds entering the Eurodollar market are available for financing multiple European investments. The MIT study for the Club of Rome,

*The Limits of Growth,* projected capital export from the Arab world reaching $200 billion over the next ten years. These long-term extrapolations are highly speculative given the changes that can occur in the political economy over that period of time, but such anticipation of trends can lead to specific policy decisions to prepare for such an eventuality.

With the intensity of the competition and the extremely low profit margins, one banker calculated that for a large bank 1¾ percent was a minimum for normal business and anything below should involve only clients who are no risk at all. But the competition is so keen that a prospective borrower will give a bank a deadline of a few hours or less to make a decision on a large loan — or he will take his business elsewhere. And the bank has no way of knowing how often or how much the borrower has already received from other banks.

"We're all basically money-market operations when you come right down to it," claimed one banker in a London branch.[12] This may have been true when all transactions were from one night to three months, and two years was con-sidered a long loan — as they were less than a decade ago. It is obviously not true today when, in response to competitive conditions, three to eight years are considered medium-term and ten-year loans are not uncommon. As competition inten-sifies, fixed interest loans have become more common while interest on deposits and interbank loans fluctuate. These loans are frequently written with no amortization procedure and with repayment in one lump sum at the end of five years, defying all minimum liquidity requirements of normal banking.

The major bankers agree that among the chief risks are that banks make loans through brokers without knowledge of the borrower, make deposits with banks of marginal standing with no information on their assets or lending plans, and lend to borrowers in foreign countries with no famil-iarity with the national legal regulations. As an example of the latter, Eurobankers frequently wrote loans to Mexicans in English, when they are legally unenforceable in Mexico unless written and signed in Spanish.

While Eurobanks make vast loans to companies and governments, the most common transactions are between the banks themselves. These deposits of deposits establish long chains and the original lender is ignorant of the subsequent use of the money, which is loaned many times. The original lender cannot know whether it is for trade, speculation, short- or long-term loans, the country, or the firm. If one link in the chain breaks, the next must make up the difference out of other reserves. But for most Eurobanks, the Eurodollar transactions are many times their capital and reserves. Nearly all the major bankers bemoan the risks and fully anticipate defaults along predictable lines which they know can lead to catastrophe. Many point to the parallels with the late twenties and early thirties. Yet all of them will continue to trade and gamble in the quest for profit.

The greatest dangers to the system are currency transfer regulations between nations and major defaults, ever present threats that mount with each transaction and the general instability of the international monetary environment. For all of these transactions are made with Eurodollars deposited for six months or less. And as one study put it, "Eurodollar deposits are the hottest of hot money . . . . At the first sign of trouble, deposits will be withdrawn quickly and in quantity."[13]

### Growing Business — And Risks

The more significant bankruptcies over the decade were momentarily sobering but failed to stem the spiral of growing risks. In 1963 the German "old, established" Hugo Stinnes Bank closed for having sinned by "lending long" and "borrowing short."[14]  In 1966 the Lebanese Intrabank failed. It had been "one of the most spectacular success stories in the annals of banking."[15]  With the reservoir of huge deposits from the oil sheiks of the Middle East, Intrabank, too, under no controls, went into "long" loans all over the world. "You don't go into real estate and airplanes with cash you have on six months deposit," scolded a British banker at the time, but today there is scarcely an international bank that since has not done the same things — or worse.[16]  While Arab oil money is notoriously volatile in seeking higher interest, it today plays an ever-greater role in the flow of Eurodollars.  Reportedly it was Libya that started dumping dollars for marks in February 1973, which touched off the crisis leading to devaluation.  It was the sudden withdrawal of Arab deposits that triggered the Intrabank collapse.  Following that collapse, for months there was much talk among bankers about a large U.S. eastern bank that was forced to sell much of its investment because of overcommitment on long-term loans in the Eurodollar market.

"Thoughts of Penn Central, Intrabank, Krupp, Rolls Royce — to mention a few — linger on," admitted the vice-president of First National City Bank of New York, the biggest operator in the business at the end of 1972.[17]  But the fact that there has not yet been the decisive crash, combined with the compulsions of the day-to-day business of making money and meeting the competition, means that despite these "thoughts," the real banking practices become ever more careless.

The collapse of the Fribgest Corporation of Lausanne, Switzerland, is illustrative of the general direction of the banking operations.  Fribgest claimed to be a subsidiary of Banque de l'Indochine in Paris and Continental Grain in New York, and on the basis of that unverified claim borrowed nearly $100 million from a number of banks. In June 1972 it collapsed with no assets, disavowed by the so-called parent corporations — Fribgest's bankers had no time to check out the facts — and left its creditors holding $68 million in paper. One bank that lent Fribgest $1.25 million had been in the Eurodollar business only two weeks and had only heard from a broker that they were "okay."[18]  Similarly, huge loans to Third World governments, already heavily in debt, are typical. The *Bankers Magazine* in its winter 1973 issue noted with relief that demand for credit was picking up for the ". . . oversupply of liquidity was to prod banks to search out new

borrowers, especially in the developing countries . . . ."[19]
The steady inflow of large deposits has further cultivated
among the bankers the belief, less and less firmly held, that
they can continue to win at the world's biggest gamble. The
profits over the past few years have been such as to encourage
their continued participation. By the summer of 1973 the
temptation of profiting between the interest differential was
intensifying the risks in banking in the U.S. as well. Some
corporations, for example, would borrow at the prime rate
of 8¾ percent and buy certificates of deposit for three months
from the same bank at 10.4 percent. Although Eurodollar
trading has been a most profitable activity for U.S. banks,
the luster has begun to tarnish and by the beginning of
1973 they could no longer conceal their anxiety over the
future: ". . . an awful lot of credit isn't going to be paid at
maturity," bleakly warned an officer of the Philadelphia
National Bank in April 1973. "There is no banker who isn't
deeply concerned," added the vice-president of Manufacturers
Hanover Trust. "Without exception we are in it, but with
deep misgivings."[20]   Alarm increased proportionately in November-December 1973 when 30 "secondary" banking houses
in London collapsed and had to be rescued, in part, quietly
by the Bank of London and a consortium of other large
banks. It was the biggest banking scandal in Britain since the
early 1930s and a portent of things to come.

### The Stock Market

This perilous international credit situation was only
compounded by the unprecedented speculation on the U.S.
stock market during the artificial "boom" of 1972, when
large investors borrowed heavily to buy cheaper-priced stocks
during the last months of the year. Since the Nixon Administration lowered the floor for margin buying to 55 percent
as an economic stimulus, margin debt rose by a record of 60
percent in 1972 — and the stock exchange index rose 23 percent. During the previous record in 1968, the margin debt
rose 24 percent and the index by 11 percent. The dangerous

implications of this increase of nearly three times the previous record, in the context of all the other factors in the world economy, are obvious. The money borrowed from the brokers rose to a record $7.9 billion in December 1972, and bank loans for market buying (and this is next to impossible to calculate) brought credit buying to an estimated minimum of $9 billion. Another new feature of the margin buying was that more debt was concentrated in fewer accounts. There was also a large increase of several billion in foreign investment in the U.S. stock market over the last months of 1972, drawn by the legendary Dow Jones average of 1,000 and the economic news that was lyrically repeating "bull market" and "economic boom."

But following the flurry of credit buying in 1972, activity on the stock market declined precipitously during 1973 when a decisive structural change in the market became evident. The foreign investors, particularly the Germans, began to reduce their holdings in large numbers after January 1973, and new investment from Europe had just about disappeared. During the first six months of 1973 member firms of the exchange, in the aggregate, made no profit and in some months more than half operated at a loss. The structural fact that underlies the plight of the stockbrokers is that the stock exchange had become what is now termed a two-tier market since the last months of 1972. And this fact had far more consequential implications for the whole economy than the profit or loss of the exchange houses.

After the recession of 1969-71, the individual investor largely withdrew from the stock market and purchases became increasingly concentrated in the hands of institutional buyers, meaning several of the largest banks and investment houses with billions of dollars to manage in trusts, pension funds, endowments, and the like. Some $330 billion of the $500 billion in American securities are in the hands of the trust departments of the nation's banks, with $139 billion concentrated in the top ten. These trust departments, long known as conservative bastions, have changed as dramatically as the currency traders making international Eurodollar loans. They have concentrated the vast capital at their disposal in approximately 50 stocks, and like traders in the international money market they move as a herd, with most banks following the lead of the top ten, and buy and sell the same stocks on the basis of advice from the same research firms. As institutional buyers comprise 70 percent of the activity on the New York Stock Exchange, those 50 stocks have accounted for most of the boom in the stock market. The favorite ten stocks get most of the attention, and while they include IBM and General Motors they also include such companies as Avon and Walt Disney. Some of the banks themselves are among the chosen few, especially Citicorp — the holding company of First National City Bank of New York. When a stock loses favor among the banks it falls like a stone, and it usually has nothing to do with its relative profitability. "The banks are putting the money in high-risk, high-multiple situations," noted one corporation executive, "so the companies get their future pension costs tied up in high risk . . . . And what's worse is they don't realize their danger."[21]

The rest of the stocks have fallen steadily or even, as in the case of some 300 in the first six months of 1973, have been withdrawn as unsalable. One broker observed that "The use of equity financings for emerging companies has not just diminished; it's ceased."[22]  In July-August 1972 there were 78 new issues; one year later there were only seven. The equity market has about dried up for many giant and highly profitable corporations as well. They have been forced to turn to the banks, and while many were willing to pay the record high rates of interest, others were not. As the chairman of Republic Steel declared, "We're not interested in maintaining a share of the industry. We're interested in profits. If that means we have to contract the company, we'll do it."[23]  The debt to equity ratios in the Standard and Poor's Industrials jumped from 26 percent to 41 percent in just a decade. Without doubt, borrowing capital instead of issuing stocks narrows falling profit margins further, even though interest rates are tax deductible. The debt is only tolerable in an expanding economy; once recessionary forces set in the across-the-economy debt is potentially devastating.

Although the trust departments of the largest banks are concentrating capital and in some cases acquiring more than 25 percent of a company's stock, one cannot make the conceptual leap, as some have done, and assume the banks are acquiring corporate control of these companies. They are playing the market in the same way and with the same motivation as the brokers would do.

The overall effect of this development in the stock market is further concentration of corporate power among those companies who can meet their needs through self-financing and borrowing. But even the giant corporations have acute liquidity crises, and given the other forces operating in the world capitalist economy the repercussions of a series of bankruptcies among medium-sized firms unable to acquire capital in a "squeeze" will be widely felt.

## The Balance-of-Payments

As recently as March 1968, just before the IMF conference, the French newspaper *Le Monde* created a storm in monetary circles by announcing that, based on quarterly figures, the U.S. would run an unheard-of deficit of $8 billion in its balance-of-payments. Yet this stunning figure paled to nothing when, just three years later, America's deficit was $22 billion on a liquidity basis and nearly $30 billion in official settlements. Like every other aspect of the U.S. in the world economy, the malaise of the payments deficit has worsened radically over the past several years so that by 1973 the total cumulative deficit had nearly doubled in two years. The pattern is clear: over the 20 years between 1950-70 the total deficit was $39.6 billion; and then in 1971-72 alone it was $40 billion — equal to the preceding 20 years. Between 1950-72 there was a deficit in every year but two — 1957 and 1968 — making a cumulative debt of $80 billion.

Such figures defy precise analysis due to multiple statistical manipulations that contribute to their inaccuracy, but some breakdown can give an indication of trends. And even the most superficial analysis underlines the unlikelihood of the Administration's proclaimed intent to reverse the balance in a couple of years, and reveals the probable effect of devaluation, import restrictions, trade offensives, and removal of capital controls on the net dollar payments position. On the other hand, the payments position could alter with a sizeable recession in the U.S., but the other problems such a pyrrhic victory would generate would make the success a very academic matter.

The official yearly balance-of-payments is composed of some 50 general categories, but the significant ones for analysis are those for trade, government expenditures, private capital flow, and errors and omissions, which all comprise the chief components of the "basic" liquidity balance. The "official government transactions" balance, on the other hand, records the U.S. debt to foreign governments, and it fluctuates wildly with the state of world confidence in the dollar. Economists generally believe that only "a reversal of recent trade trends" holds any hope for modifying the balance-of-payments deficit that is now a characteristic of the U.S. economy.[24]

The trade deficit, as I discussed in Chapter Two, in the official understated figures was $6.8 billion in 1972, three times the record of the previous year. Many had expected an improvement rather than deterioration after the devaluation of December 1971. In part, one deficit reflected increases in the price of imported goods because of the new currency parities, and to a greater degree it was due to the generally booming U.S. economy in 1972. The balance-of-trade deteriorated with every part of the world save the centrally planned economies of the U.S.S.R., Eastern Europe, and China. Trade with Canada, Germany, and Japan accounted for most of the deficit, and the deficit with both Germany and Japan had increased by more than one-third. In 1960-62 trade with those three countries accounted for 30 percent of the American trade surplus. The only gain in the balance was in agricultural commodities, such as grain sales principally to the U.S.S.R., rose 32 percent.

Government subsidies and intracorporate trade account for a good part of the exports, and it is open to question if there would be a significant market at all for much of American exports if it were not for the intercession of the government or corporations. It can be argued that what is important is the effect of these foreign orders on the American economy, irrespective of who ultimately pays and when. But for assessing payments balances, and the continued presence of dollars abroad, such facts mean that the trade figures have even less bearing than is generally assumed. In 1968 fully one-third of American exports were financed by government or intracompany credits which may never be paid by a transfer of dollars but are merely bookkeeping entries. According to a detailed study by Michael Hudson, if actual payments (the inflow of currency or even barter of goods) were calculated, as was the case before World War II, the 1968 trade balance would have been a deficit of $5.1 billion rather than the officially proclaimed surplus of $0.6 billion. In 1970 Secretary of Commerce Stans pointed out that the trade surplus in agriculture would be eliminated if the government's Food-for-Peace (PL-480) and similar programs did not exist.[25] Price controls in the U.S., as in 1973 on industrial supplies, chemicals, and the like, mean that the U.S. producers will seek the higher prices abroad and be in a position to compete. There can be a temporary shift in the trade balance based on such factors coupled with a devaluation, but the structural factors are not altered and others will not abandon the competitive struggle.

Government expenditures abroad, with long-term private capital outflow, compose the largest negative figure in the balance of "invisibles." Military spending, of course, makes up the largest proportion of the government expenditures, and has been a significant cause of the balance-of-payments deficit. In 1971 military outlays abroad exceeded sales of military equipment by nearly $3 billion. In 1972 that deficit increased by more than $500 million. These military expenditures abroad of $4.8 billion in 1971 were relatively unchanged over 1969 and 1970. Wages and salaries for both the U.S. military and foreign workers accounted for 50 percent of that figure. Procurement of major equipment amounted to $150 million, and materials and supplies were $700 million, of which $440 million was for petroleum. Most of the expenditures were in Germany — $1.2 billion — followed by $600 million in Japan, $520 million in Vietnam, and over $300 million in Korea. Offshore procurement for military assistance, once the largest component in military spending abroad, peaking at $640 million in 1955, was only $4 million by 1971. Military grants to foreign governments amounted to $3.2 billion. Government grants, excluding military, were more than $2 billion.

These expenditures must be balanced by trade, repatriated profits, or new investment by foreigners in the U.S. Most corporations are now reluctant to repatriate their profits from the hard currency areas as there remains little incentive to hold dollars. Some continue to meet the mandatory requirements by borrowing Eurodollars just prior to the year's deadline and repaying the loan just after. Nevertheless, by far the largest credit in the entire ledger is the repatriated profit and interest and dividend income from private foreign investment, which in 1972 returned $13.5 billion. But the net balance declined over 1971 as foreign repatriation of interest and dividends from the U.S. increased by $750 million to a total of $6 billion. There was a reduction in long-term capital outflow for direct investment as the U.S. corporations borrowed abroad for their needs through bond issues or banks, increasing their foreign debt during 1972 by $3.2 billion. Foreign investment income could not compensate, however, for the capital outflows from government and private sources as well as the trade deficit.

The "errors and omissions" category in the balance-of-payments is used to cover the growth of dollars abroad that cannot be explained by trade, investment, or expenditures. As the deficit in that category shot up from $1 billion in 1970 to $11 billion in 1971 it obviously refers to the unreported capital flow due to the periodic dollar crises and the huge increase in holdings of dollars abroad. Figures declined in 1972 but were again swollen in 1973 due to the dollar crisis of February, when "errors and omissions" and bank transfers were $8.2 billion in the first quarter of that year.

The "official settlements" balance represents the claim of the central banks of foreign governments on the U.S. government itself as additional dollars amassed over the years. After reaching a staggering $30 billion in 1971, necessitating Nixon's decision to make the dollar nonconvertible, in 1972 the deficit subsided to $10.1 billion, or equal to its previous record high of 1970. But in 1973 the official deficit was again $10.5 billion in the first quarter alone. As foreign governments can no longer convert the dollars into gold or other reserves, they bought marketable U.S. government securities or Treasury nonmarketable short- and medium-term bonds, and they also increased their official deposits with American banks.

During the dollar crisis of 1973, Washington actually welcomed the massive influx of nonconvertible dollars from the German central bank in exchange for IOUs. Since the U.S. is in debt at every level of its economic activity, the dollars relieved the government from being forced to turn to the private capital market for funds to finance the internal deficit at a time when it was trying to hold a check on interest rates. It is important to remember in this regard that the government does not simply print money to pay for its deficit, but borrows in the capital markets in competition with private capitalists. The Federal government is the nation's prime borrower, and in 1971 it borrowed $26 billion in the private capital market, and at the end of that year U.S. government marketable securities made up 15 percent of all securities in the U.S. State and local governments also compete and are usually the first "squeezed" in a recession. Government agencies, such as the General Services Administration, often independently float their own certificates. The budget deficit which must be covered by these competitive borrowings represents a real threat to private capitalists during a period of tight credit. In 1972 the public debt comprised 25 percent of the total debt in the U.S. of $2.5 trillion.[26]

There is little reason to believe that devaluation will change the U.S. predicament. In Europe the change in the parity of currencies can have a real effect on the trade and payments balance because trade is such an important part of the economic activity. For America, other elements are paramount, and shift of parities, except on a massive scale, will not bring about a substantial shift in a deficit which reflects other factors. For this reason, as one Italian central banker has noted, the world was better off when sterling was the reserve currency since it was more sensitive to the currents of trade. Furthermore, there is nothing to prevent competitive devaluations as in the 1930s, or other shifts in government restrictions on trade if adverse effects are felt in other parts of the world. As for U.S. government expenditures, the devaluation will only increase its costs. But all this is simply a reflection of the real forces operating in the world economy, and these are fundamental questions of profitability and confidence.

The skyrocketing price of gold is only a barometer of this growing lack of confidence in paper money and the economy in general. Since all governments accept gold without reservation in intergovernment payments the mystique of gold is strong enough to attract sufficient cash from around the world, and once the pace of a price rise quickens, gold, like any commodity or securities, attracts large flows of cash. The nonconvertible dollars are now weighing heavily on those nations in debt to the IMF. The Fund filled its quota of dollars and yet many nations can only pay their debts with their dollar reserves. Before August 1971 they would simply turn them in to the U.S. Treasury for gold or another hard currency. No longer possible, they must sell their dollars for another currency such as marks, increasing the pressure on the German or another economy, or not pay their debts — which would shortly bring the IMF system to a halt.

As America's supply of gold dwindled and it became clear it was running out of other reserve assets with the IMF, the U.S. pressed in that organization for the invention of a new paper money — the Special Drawing Rights (SDRs) — to meet its own demands for liquidity in other currencies, and talked loudly, but ineffectually, on the subject of de-monetizing gold. Allocations of the original SDR creation of $9.5 billion worth were made on the basis of the initial contributions to the Fund, thereby giving the U.S. the largest share. That three-year initial division was not adequate for the American needs and the U.S. pressed for the allocation of new issues. The other members, principally the French, successfully resisted this stratagem. In 1973, on the other hand, at the annual meeting of the IMF and World Bank, the Third World countries demanded a greater share of the SDRs for their development needs. Secretary of the Treasury George Shultz bitterly opposed this position, claiming it would undermine confidence in the SDRs and create more liquidity than the world needed. What he really meant was that there would be more than the U.S. required.[27] For the IMF had created the SDRs only to meet America's desperate debt and not to alleviate the plight of other nations.

One of the critical ambiguities of the international capitalist system today is that the role of the dollar and the U.S. economy is both a serious plague to the stability of world capitalism as well as a significant stimulant to it. It is a fact that the dollar contributed liquidity throughout the world, and exports to the U.S. market created a prosperity, however spurious, especially for Germany and Japan. And the prosperity in Germany — largely dependent on both sales to the U.S. and the inflow of dollars through military expenditures or speculation — was of great importance to the rest of Europe and to those nations from which it recruited workers. At the same time it increased the costs for German capitalism. In short, underlying trends created a movement toward fundamental crisis in the political economy in Europe and Japan as well. The ramifications of these trends I discuss in greater detail in the next chapter.

Monetary negotiations, like most diplomacy in general, are merely stagecraft, and an aspect of trade war. Arrangements can only reflect power relations which are currently in flux. The U.S. is no longer in unchallenged dominance in the world economy, but neither has it yet met its equal. But since there is no omnipotent superpower to impose new regulations on the world economy, all diplomatic efforts to regulate it will fail. The collapse of this fragile world economy will come, and it has already begun, through the internal dynamics of the capitalist system itself, which concentrates world resources and financial power and yet acts competitively through the imperatives of the immediate interests of each individual, corporation and nation moving to avoid loss or gain profit.

### CHAPTER FOUR

## DILEMMAS OF THE "ECONOMIC MIRACLES"
## OF THE INDUSTRIAL NATIONS

Viewed from the day-to-day perspective, there is never a peaceful period of economic growth and development; there is always turmoil and conflict. Seen from the vantage of a few years, economists and others can, and do, retrospectively round off the jagged corners and generalize on trends in the economies in the world by tallying up statistics and projecting their findings into the future. In the early 1960s this led to many books speculating on the economic growth in the West and Japan, concluding that capitalism had solved its dilemmas and could march into the future with the same steady progress of the preceding decade.[1]

With the repetition of the headline-making monetary crises, successive devaluations, record trade and budget deficits, less-than-amiable confrontations among old allies, war and recessions, observers are no longer as ready to generalize on the permanence of American capitalist prosperity. Attention then focused on the fact that the U.S. is no longer the unchallenged economic power in the capitalist world; and that the EEC and Japan now stand as bastions of economic strength. It is indeed facile to say that the EEC and Japan are strong industrial powers because of their industrial plant and production, but it is more significant to examine the origins of their remarkable growth and their prospects for the future. With the escalation of oil prices by four times over 1973 the vulnerability of these economies became more evident, but there is still a need to comprehend *all* the forces affecting both their remarkable past growth and their current crisis.

Putting aside the questions of concentration of corporate control and the fragile world credit structure discussed in Chapters Two and Three, in this chapter I would like to explore several of the other closely linked structural dilemmas in the industrial capitalist states, focusing primarily on the economic "miracle" nations — West Germany, Italy, and Japan.

To fully understand the vulnerability of these powers in the context of world capitalism it is important to examine the origins of their post-war economic growth, the contradictions that exist on nearly every level of economic activity, and the crisis-provoking responses to their new challenges from the capitalists themselves. Finally, we must note how the role of capitalist "planning," or the persistent effort to control or modify economic crises of inflation or recession by the introduction of orthodox fiscal and monetary economic principles in a national or international context, contributes to the general instability of the world capitalist economy.

One cannot pretend in a short study to do justice to all the components of an industrial capitalism, but the complexities need not hide certain, too often overlooked, causal factors in the remarkable growth rates of the German, Italian, and Japanese economies.

West Germany remains the key to the Western European economy. It produces 40 percent of Western Europe's (excluding Britain) products and is the largest market. The West German economy is also the most intimately linked to the U.S. of any on the continent through government expenditures, private investment, and trade. Its economic prosperity — or decline — has an immediate impact on the rest of Europe, for whom it is by far the largest market which has accounted for much of the EEC economic expansion, for, as I have noted before, the domino analogy has much more validity in economics than in politics. One of the most

industrial nations in the world, West German industry contributes 54 percent of the GNP compared to 36 percent for
the United States. Investment expenditures for capital goods
has been the focus of economic growth. Between 1948 and
1957 its growth rate at 8 percent was the highest in Western
Europe and its GNP doubled between 1952 and 1960. It was
only after 1958, however, that "boom" conditions characterized the economy.[2]

The Italian economy won the designation of "economic
miracle" because of its remarkable overall growth of 7.8 percent annually between 1954-70, and an industrial growth
rate which averaged 9 percent between 1950 and 1958 and
11 percent between 1958 and 1961. Starting from a relatively low base, the Italians built an advanced industrial belt
across northern Italy specializing in autos, large electrical
consumer appliances, and chemicals. Consumer durable
production, one symbol of Italian growth, was an entirely
postwar phenomenon, but the real growth industries were
also in the capital goods sector.

Italy between 1955 and 1969 has been likened to the
"Roaring Twenties" in the U.S. It was a period of rapid
social mobility for a few, sharp acceleration in the concentration of capital, the proletarianization of agricultural workers
from the South, unbridled pollution of the physical environment, and massive adulteration of food and drugs. Small
entrepreneurs, such as Ignis refrigerators, boomed into big
industry in a few years, and the older big capitalists, like
Agnelli of Fiat, Cinzano, and others diversified into industrial empires. The public and semi-public corporations, in
1970 comprising 25 percent of the gross fixed investment
and run exactly like private industry, have been unable to
play a decisive role in the direction of the economy, or to
maintain growth after 1969.[3]

Japan, perhaps better than any other nation on earth,
represents the quintessence of the capitalist ethic as well as
the contradictions and illusions of strength which, in reality,
hid fundamental weakness. In 20 years Japan has succeeded
in becoming the third-ranking industrial power in the world

in output, after the U.S. and the U.S.S.R., but only number 18 in per capita income. Yet in terms of annual growth of its GNP it has been number one, averaging 9.4 percent between 1953 and 1965, and increasing the rate to 12 percent by 1968 and maintaining roughly this level in the subsequent years. On an industry-by-industry basis, Japan is the world leader in such fields as shipbuilding — with 47.5 percent of the world's total output — motorcycles, sewing machines, transistor radios, and certain types of steel. It ranks second place in textiles, newsprint, synthetic rubber, steel, aluminum, and automobiles. Such advances in growth were not steady over this period but were accompanied by wide fluctuations in the business cycle, considerably more intense than in the other industrial countries and each time wiping out numerous small companies and further concentrating capital. Such cycles were generally manipulated by the government at times of heavy balance-of-payments deficits in the late 1950s and 1960s.[4]

Although certain events and conditions of national economies are readily comprehensible by a careful scrutiny of material forces, there is a tendency among economists and other academics to generalize on trends, to project contemporary conditions into the future isolated from the very causal factors in world capitalism that continue to operate. This has been especially true in superficial analyses of the Japanese economy that attribute its success to cultural factors, racial theories, or projections on the future of Japanese power — all ideological explanations divorced from the quite materialist evidence of the past as well as from the vulnerability of the Japanese economy to the forces operating in the world economy today. The rest of the world will not stand still while the Japanese economy continues to march upward as it has over the past decade. Its success has been inseparable from external factors, and those are in a state of constant change. This is not to dismiss unique cultural ingredients altogether in economic development, but it is to point out that they are minor and once the economic environment of world capitalism changes that will become vividly clear to all. The Japanese economy is one of the most vulnerable in the world today. The impact of the oil crisis in 1973-74 made this vulnerability obvious to all, but there is considerably more involved than Japan's dependence on oil imports, a fact that was always understood. The crisis in reserves and supplies only highlighted the multiple factors at play in Japanese capitalism.

## The Origins of Growth

Despite the rather contrived explanations by many bourgeois economists, the rapid accumulation of capital over the two postwar decades rested on five principal (and what should be obvious) factors operating in the world economy: the political events of the time — primarily war and the preparation for war, artificial capital liquidity based on the role of the dollar in foreign investment and trade, a relatively passive and migratory working class in part recruited from the agricultural population or the underdeveloped countries on the fringe of industrial Europe, the direct role of credit in capital expansion, and an industrial base that was dependent on export markets. These factors, discussed in detail below, were not static but were in the process of constant change as they were affected by other elements operating in the world economy. All of these ingredients make the economies involved extremely vulnerable to quite uncontrollable events outside their national boundaries and none of the real causal factors in the "miracle" economies' growth rates depended on domestic features within the control of the government or industrial leaders involved.

### The Political Context

It is impossible to discuss the phenomenal growth of the European and Japanese economies in a vacuum of economic data divorced from the most important political events in the world at the time. Yet, astonishingly, this has been all too common in economists' discussions of these economies over the past decades, as "the advent of the rather permanent crisis conditions" were "oddly celebrated as the taming of the business-cycle via conscious interference in the market mechanism" — as Paul Mattick observed in 1969.[5]  For paramount in their entire development was the political fact of war and the preparation for war on the part of the U.S., the dominant capitalist power at the time of the European and Japanese economic growth.  This reality established the steady demand for their goods and services, directly and indirectly sustaining their continued high level of production.

The Korean war and its economic and political aftermath had the decisive effect on the growth of Germany and Japan, pulling both out of a systemic stagnation and setting their course for the subsequent decades.  The impact of that war, discussed at length in *The Limits of Power,* resulted in a fundamental restructuring of global markets as the former Axis powers were able to meet the world demand for industrial and consumer goods while the victorious Allies oriented their economies toward production of war materials and arms.

After 1954, the "Cold War" atmosphere was essential to the continued government export of dollars as U.S. military expenditures and offshore procurement programs continued to infuse liquidity and artificial demand into West Germany and Japan.  Between 1946 and 1958 the U.S. government aid and loan programs alone to Western Europe amounted to $25 billion, and Japan received $3.8 billion during 1945-64. West Germany reached its prewar output in 1951, but reconstruction continued to be an important aspect of Japan's growth rate until 1959.

A widely noted feature in the Japanese trade and industrial "miracle" was the absence of waste expenditures for military and space programs.  Japan spent $963 million in contrast to the U.S. expenditure of $67.4 billion in 1966-67, or only 7.2 of its 1969 government budget, as opposed to 42.5 percent in 1968 for the U.S.  Such facts, however, are less important than generally assumed, for one of the most critical elements in the entire postwar Japanese economic experience has been its parasitic relationship to a U.S. economy that was profoundly affected by massive expenditures on two wars in Asia, plus a special procurement agreement negotiated in 1954 whereby the U.S. would buy hundreds of millions of dollars worth of goods and services for its imperialist adventures in Asia. Simultaneously, Japan was able to pick up markets from the British while they too were diverted by arms programs in Europe during the 1950s. The great turning points of the Japanese economy, for both its intimately linked foreign trade and internal development, were the Korean and Vietnam wars. In 1953 U.S. troop expenditures paid for one-third of Japanese imports and U.S. procurement paid for 60 percent of Japan's exports. More important than the direct procurement orders was the expansion of the U.S. and world markets as a result of the American war economy. Between 1965 and 1967 Japanese trade grew by 80 percent and its trade with the U.S. by 100 percent. It has been estimated that American purchases directly arising from the Vietnam war totaled 10 percent of Japanese exports. And between 1967 and 1970 Japan increased its share of world export trade by one-third, in large part because of the preoccupations and diversionary military orders that were distracting the American corporations from meeting domestic consumer demand or competing in the world markets. As a National City Bank analysis pointed out, "the Japanese economy could not have soared so persistently unless it had been propelled by continuous increases in demand." And that steady demand was provided by foreign markets which in turn were stimulated by wars in both Korea and Vietnam. This foreign market through the 1960s, fostered directly and indirectly by the American war in Indochina, ". . .compensated for cyclical fluctuations" in domestic demand and ". . . provided alternative markets for the output of Japan's high growth industries. . . ."[6] It is not too much to assume that as long as Japan's businessmen can profit by peacefully selling, and can retain access to their vital raw material supplies, they will not be interested in wasteful military expenditures. If or when there is a serious internal crisis due to restricted foreign markets or raw materials, the role of military expenditures will increase accordingly, precisely as they have done in the United States.

Not unlike the symbiotic Japanese-American relationship, German exports to the U.S. increased between 1965 and 1970 by nearly 2.5 times, compared to a rise of only 33 percent over the previous 5 years. And it was the escalation of war in Indochina in 1967-68 that pulled Germany out of its most serious recession since 1950. Subsequently, the escalation in 1972 cut short the impending recession in that year.

### Role of Foreign Investment

Also stimulating the economic growth in Europe, as I discussed in Chapters Two and Three, was the influx of dollars via private U.S. investment after 1958. The differential in the rate of profit, which in Germany was twice as high as the U.S. after 1954, and the organization of the EEC were the critical attractions of the private dollar inflow that added considerable fuel to economic growth. In Italy the influx of foreign capital, principally dollars, became a "torrent," increasing five times between 1957 and 1961. Seventy-five percent of American investment to 1970 was in metallurgy, petroleum, chemicals, and electronics — the high growth industries of northern Italy. And the greater Western Europe's growth and profit, the more their economies attracted further capital. As the UN Economic Commission for Europe (ECE) observed, "These funds . . . helped to provide international liquidity to facilitate the growth of trade and output in Western Europe."[7]

Foreign direct investment played a very small role in Japan. Only the American oil companies have dominated the entire industry in Japan since the occupation. As a consequence, Japanese own only 10 percent of the oil used in Japan. It was one of the few industries interested in taking advantage of the U.S. occupation to achieve a dominant position in the Japanese economy. The manufacturing industries in autos, electronics, cameras, and the like, may regret it today, but at the time of their unique opportunity they were simply not interested in investing in a devastated Japan. When it was profitable, it was too late.

Instead of admitting direct investment, Japanese capitalism was able to profit to an extraordinary degree by scouting out and incorporating technological innovations from around the world, but principally the U.S. — innovations that were largely the outcome of military research and development.[8] Between 1950-69, Japan paid $1.5 billion in royalties and licenses for U.S. technology that cost the Americans up to $20 billion a year in research and development. It is important to note in this regard that the Japanese have now exhausted the backlog of world technology, so that important factor in their growth will not be repeated. The Japanese, recognizing this fact, have finally begun to channel significant investment into basic research.

## The Working Class

The phenomenal growth in both Europe and Japan over the past two decades was possible in great part because of the relatively quiescent working class. Unemployment in Germany, Belgium, and Denmark ranged between 5-10 percent in the mid-1950s. In Italy it was over 10 percent throughout that decade. In Italy and Japan the process of absorbing a large number of unemployed, or the transfer of workers from agriculture to industry, facilitated their extraordinary growth rates. In Japan, between 1953 and 1970 the number of workers in agriculture fell from 42 percent to 20 percent. In Italy the high unemployment and the recruitment of workers from the south were inhibiting factors on the working class demands in the 1950s and early 1960s — the period of the Italian "miracle." The first big change in employment occurred in 1960 when a labor shortage in some sectors developed as an outcome of the massive increase in exports. In 1960 the northern industries began to absorb southern workers and the increase in employment in that year alone equalled the entire preceding decade. Wages rose substantially between 1961 and 1964 as Italy lost what some economists have called the unemployment "advantage."[9] Yet throughout the "boom" years, Italy had the lowest overall labor costs in the EEC.

In West Germany, the growth of the 1950s was also able to absorb a substantial German unemployment, and during the 1960s workers were recruited in large numbers from the Mediterranean countries where unemployment on a large scale is characteristic. The recruitment began in 1956, and there were one million foreign workers by 1964 and double that by 1971, or 8.2 percent of the total. The numbers vary with the business cycle, of course, and it has been an important safety valve in the economy. Throughout the period of accelerated growth, the German working class was reputed for its tranquillity on every level — what *Business Week,* referring to the machine tool industry, called the "cornerstone of the West German . . . phenomenal growth. . . ."[10] Between 1956 and 1961 only 29 days per year of 1,000 workers were lost in strikes as compared to 187 days in Britain. During this period West Germany built the foundation of its trade surplus as low wages held down domestic demand for substantial imports and kept German products competitive. Further curtailing consumption of the working class, the Government relied on sales and consumption taxes for its revenue.

Over the postwar decades the unions have played an important role in the stability of European capitalism. In Italy, they were highly centralized and primarily Communist party controlled, and industry expected steady, predictable and moderate wage gains for the organized but was spared costly "work rule" concessions on a local level. A significant dual wage system evolved between the organized and unorganized, chiefly reflecting the size of the industry — with the organized concentrated in the largest industries. In the early 1960s 30 percent of the employed Italians worked in companies of ten workers or less.

In West Germany the unions were integrated into the codetermination management schemes whose effect was to give the union leaders a sense of "responsibility" in keeping workers' demands at a low keyed and predictable level. The German capitalists had accepted the scheme as a "reasonable price to pay for a relatively strike-free life. . . ."[11]

There are an estimated 9 million immigrant workers in the EEC countries today. They have played a critical role in the rapid growth of the European economies by filling a large need for unskilled workers and they "dampened wages" for more than a decade.

In Japan, as well, a primary cause of accelerated growth was an exceptionally high degree of exploitation of the Japanese working class, which is highly skilled and whose technical education ranks ahead of both the U.S. and Europe. Most factories in Japan never stop, operating 24 hours a day, 365 days a year. Between 1965-70 productivity growth was 14.2 percent while unit labor cost rose by only 0.8 percent.[12]

## The Role of Credit Finance

Particularly in Germany and Japan, industries have relied heavily on external credit for economic growth, making the superficially powerful economies extremely vulnerable to cyclical developments.

The credit financing of the German economy was based on the expectation that the upward trend in the economy would be permanent, and between 1954 and 1966 this assumption, from their perspective, appeared justified. Only a "small part" of the working capital of German industry is generated internally or through the stock market. But as the massive infusion of dollars contributed inflation as well as prosperity, the government of orthodox economist Ludwig Erhard introduced deflationary policies in 1966 "to balance the budget, stop inflation, boost exports," and he tightened German credit.[13]

The credit restrictions only partially achieved their purpose since the German corporations were heavily in debt to foreign banks. By the end of September 1966 their gross foreign debt was DM23 billion, and their net indebtedness was over DM4 billion. In addition, more than one-half this debt was concentrated in the subsidiaries of U.S. corporations.

But by March 1967 Erhard's policies in large part achieved some effect. Insolvencies of companies with assets over DM1 million increased by 80 percent. These bankruptcies revealed how far much of the postwar economy had been financed with borrowed capital. The assets of one large company that collapsed in 1967 were only 6 to 8 percent of its total debts. The sharp recession, leading to a financial crisis within the Krupp empire as well, provided a reminder of the fragile foundation of even the older components of the German economy.

During the first week of March 1967 the giant Krupp industrial empire, one of Germany's top ten, employing 110,000 workers and with $1.2 billion in annual sales, had to be "humiliatingly rescued," according to the *Economist,* with DM600 million from the German government and the biggest banks.[14]   Four-fifths of its working capital was borrowed money and one-half of its debt was in short-term bank loans continually rescheduled. This fixed-interest debt to over 200 banks and credit organizations meant a crisis when the economy entered a recession. The bankers were unwilling to loan more and the company had to turn to the government for guarantees. It was not until the winter of 1970, after considerable restructuring, that the corporation again operated at a profit. As of mid-1973 a principal characteristic of German industry, and one that inhibited many companies from expanding overseas, was that debt continued to comprise two-thirds of working capital.[15]

In Italy, credits to private industry increased 612 percent between 1948 and 1961, and accounted for more than one-fifth of total manufacturing investment — with heavy concentration in the large corporations. After 1957 the general inflow of dollars added to the lending capacity of the banks. The "miracle" years of 1958-61 were dependent on massive credits from both private and public sources, Italian and foreign.[16]

The impressive Japanese industrial machine rests on such fragile props as well. The pattern of financing investment and subsequent growth in Japan parallels trends in the U.S. and Europe. Before the war, 50 percent of corporate funds were generated internally; by the mid-1950s the proportion had fallen to 30 percent and in 1969 the figure had reached 22 percent. Interest payments on borrowed capital

are heavy. Close to 100 percent of Japanese bank deposits
are loaned, principally for investment. In 1968 all the largest
industries were heavily in debt in a very fragile structure of
industry in debt to banks which in turn were indebted to
the central bank and to the banks of New York. Many
loans in the 1950s were suppliers' credits from corporations,
such as General Electric and Westinghouse, to Japanese
power companies. The World Bank loaned to auto and
shipbuilding corporations as well as such projects as hydro-
electric dams. As Japanese industry moved abroad, 85 percent of the capital invested was borrowed — loans guaranteed
by the central bank. The Bank of Japan has played a critical
role, financing much of the high growth industry by guaran-
teeing, principally to the New York finance market, loans
otherwise impossible to attain. As one observer pointed out,
the impact of an international economic crisis could set the
whole structure crumbling like "a castle of cards."[17]


## The Role of Exports

Linked to all of the above factors and fundamental to
their economic growth, has been the export orientation of
basic industry within the German, Italian, and Japanese economies. Through the 1950s and 1960s German basic industries
— VW, Krupp, chemicals, machine tools, and the like — relied
on exports to the U.S. and Europe for 40 to 50 percent of
their sales. Of the top 50 industries in Germany, 13 rely on
foreign sales for more than 40 percent of their earnings but
six of them number in the top ten. Export markets were the
key to expansion and, especially in times of crisis, were able
to pull the German economy out of recession. It was Krupp's
overriding dependence on export sales that necessitated the
continued expansion of long-term credits to its customers in
the highly competitive foreign markets, and which in turn
led to its near bankruptcy in 1967. But as 1967-68 were
years of upsurge in the U.S. economy due to the escalation
of the war in Vietnam, foreign orders were sufficient to pull
the German economy out of its recession, as they did again

in 1972. The role of foreign sales was assessed by the president of the Federation of German Industry: "Thanks to our *exports* — which amount to one-fifth of the Federal Republic of Germany's industrial output — the recent recession was relatively mild and short."[18]  By 1970, VW, Germany's largest corporation, depended on foreign sales for 69 percent of its total income, and 40 percent of its German production was exported. This heavy dependence of basic German industry is one of the most vulnerable characteristics of the entire economy.

In Italy exports accounted for 18.5 percent of the GNP in the "miracle" years but for a much greater percentage of the major industries of the country — autos, chemicals, iron, and steel. The money supply based on foreign reserves from export sales and foreign investment increased, adding further stimulus to the economy. The organization of the EEC was extremely important as the exports to the region grew 63 percent between 1958 and 1961. The entire consumer industry was geared to exports to the rest of Europe. Producing 48 percent of Europe's refrigerators and 36 percent of its washing machines, the expanding market of the 1950s and 1960s — consumption in Western Europe rose an average of 4.5 percent a year over the period — was a major contribution to the success of Italian capitalism. But as one does not often buy a refrigerator, the backlog of demand generated by the rapid economic growth throughout Europe was saturated by 1970.[19]

*Le Monde* correspondent Robert Guillain asserted in his comprehensive study of Japan that it is a myth to believe world trade is the motor of the Japanese economy. The internal market is the primary origin of profit. Exports are to pay for essential imports of raw materials to produce primarily for the Japanese themselves. Exports account for only 10 percent of Japanese production by contrast to 32 percent for Holland, 15 percent for Britain, and 20 percent for Germany. A major change in its export trade since the prewar period has been the rise in capital goods exports. Before the war textiles made up one-half of the exports and they now account for less than 20 percent. And this share of foreign trade in the GNP is only one-half that of 1937.

Although these observations are interesting and contradict the popular impression of the Japanese economy's being wholly geared to trade, one should, nevertheless, be wary of carrying them too far, not merely regarding the Japanese but similar generalizations on the American economy as well. Beside the obvious fact that Japan is wholly dependent on imports for raw materials, what is significant is the political and economic power of the industries which make up that 10 percent and the importance of the trade sector to *their* total growth and profit. This is far more interesting in understanding the dynamics of any economy than the compilation of the economic activity of the millions of marginal producers of goods and services that do exist in Japan as well as those whom Guillain calls the "vast world of the useless," but which also makes up an important part of the GNP.[20] What is important is not just that trade was critical to these economies and to their postwar growth, but rather what was the origin of the postwar demand for their exports. And this originated with the stimulus of the war spending in the U.S., the dominant capitalist state.

### Contradictions, Conflict, and Change

By the end of 1968 it should have been evident to most economic decision-makers that new developments would radically alter the economic environment of nearly two decades of growth. The corroding dilemma of inflation, the acute monetary crisis, the new role of the working class, and the sharpened competitive struggle for markets changed the calculations of those whose judgments can alter the economy.

As noted in Chapter Three, the U.S. economy was essentially a two-edged sword for the European and Japanese economies, providing both an infusion of capital and the stimulant of a large aggregate demand; but it was also an inflationary force to which they responded with crisis-inducing, deflationary measures and other, rather irrelevant, orthodox economic policies. A preoccupation with the problem in Europe, according to a UN survey, had inhibited many expansionary policies between 1950 and 1970. Attempts to compensate for the inflation by raising interest rates only attracted new short-term capital. Increasingly, only extreme measures of this nature would have any effect, and then only at the cost of a guaranteed crisis. But the effectiveness of manipulating interest rates was largely eliminated from the repertoire of the capitalist governments due to their cherished freedom of capital movement and the role of the dollar. But the failure of the old monetary techniques led to their more drastic, record setting application with each successive crisis.

### Renewed Working Class Militancy

The role of the working class has changed radically over the past five years from the standpoint of the decision-making capitalists and government leaders themselves. And their response to this change and their calculations and plans can transform militant working class action on a local level into an ingredient that further undermines the foundation of the economy and that can further aggravate social conflict and set in motion a set of events whose outcome cannot be anticipated by anyone.

By the end of the 1960s, the workers throughout Europe were no longer willing to produce and to pay in relative silence, and one group of European capitalists after another faced prolonged strikes — usually of a wildcat nature — and were forced to grant within several years the pay increases denied over the previous decades. In Japan there was considerable competition for workers in the late 1960s and the wages for the average industrial worker rose at 16-17 percent a year. At the same time vast numbers of the unorganized in the two-tier labor market got little and were merely squeezed by the mounting inflation. The wages of those companies employing 100 or fewer workers are less than 50 percent of those employing 1,000 or more. Starting with the general strike in France in May 1968, an event that surprised everyone, French capitalists experienced increased labor costs, political turmoil, capital outflow, inflationary pressures, and a devaluation of the franc. In the following years the other European capitalists also became locked in costly confrontations with the workers.

In Italy, the fall of 1969 became known as the "hot autumn" as militant workers closed one industry after the other across the industrial belt of the north, forcing large pay increases, which rose an average of 18 percent in 1970. By 1973 the average Fiat worker was making 50 percent more than 1969. Labor's new role of continued agitation, absenteeism, and periodic wildcat strikes led to profound changes in the calculations of Italian capitalists.

By 1969 the "tranquility" in West Germany had also come to an end, starting with the wildcat strikes in the steel industry which then spread to the other major industries in the country. As a result, wages were forced up more than 50 percent in the processing industries between 1969 and mid-1972. The auto workers won a 40 percent increase over the same period. By the fall of 1973 wildcat strikes, most with active participation of the foreign workers, were becoming steadily more common in West Germany. Even Volkswagen in Wolfesburg, where worker militancy was unknown in 35 years, was shaken in April 1973, and fanned fears among the managers that VW may in its turn become a center of social agitation comparable to Renault near Paris. And this assessment of a transformation in the German working class has become an important input in the decisions of the German industrialists.

In England, despite, and because of, the government's best efforts to "discipline" the British workers to enhance the competitiveness of the British economy in preparation for entry into the Common Market, there was a steady succession of militant wildcat strikes in one industry after the other between 1971 and 1972, and at the end of 1973 it was the conflict between the workers and the state, rather than the oil crisis, which had the most critical impact on the British economy.

At the same time, the role of the migrant worker is rapidly changing in the eyes of the European industrialist.

There is no longer any guarantee that this "safety valve" will continue to operate in a profitable way. The costs of recruiting workers and the requirements of the state for training them have all become considerably more costly over the past few years. In France and Germany the immigrant worker is increasingly in the forefront in strikes. Between 1968 and 1972 the hourly compensation and unit labor costs in West Europe and Japan reflected the new pressure. Unit labor cost rose in 1970 over 1969 in Germany by 12.3 percent, in Italy by 14.4 percent, in Japan by 7 percent, in contrast to the U.S. and Canada, where it rose 6 percent.

More disturbing than the cost factor of higher wages, which can often be passed on again through inflation (though not as easily as before due to the mounting competition for a limited market), are the politically and economically destabilizing wildcat nature of the strikes. The ability of the unions to perform their historic role as a means of disciplining labor has diminished sharply throughout Europe since May 1968, and is now a source of alarm among European capitalists. In mid-1973 a favorite story among Italian businessmen is of the plant executive who said, "I wish to hell the Communists took over Italy. They alone can make those bastards work."[21] Comments such as these came at a time when the Communist party was trying again to curb labor agitation and strikes throughout the country.

In France the CP and its unions, unwilling to be in the tail of the rank-and-file activity as in May 1968, publicly, if reluctantly, support the demands of the workers even though they do not initiate them. Even so, they rarely comprehend or appreciate the nature of the issue. At Renault the foreign workers made nonwage demands and when the company offered a wage increase the Communists hailed it a victory and the workers rejected the offer. Throughout Western Europe the conflict between the workers and the trade unions, wedded to periodic and rigid contracts, is intensifying. The unions, like the companies, see the "leftist outside agitator" as a principal cause of the problem.

Increasingly, the demands in Europe are of a nonwage

nature and are not so easily met in a capitalist context. The universal expression of these new nonwage claims prompted the OECD to call a meeting of corporate executives in 1972 to discuss possible solutions. Their consensus was that, throughout Europe and even Japan, the workers' question, "What right has this person to give me orders?" characterized their new challenge.[22] This continual agitation among the workers is an important calculation for European capitalists in their urgent search for competitive advantages to restore profitable growth. As trade competition intensifies, passing on costs through inflation is no longer so acceptable, especially in industries with one-half or more of production for export, industries whose sales are also undermined by fluctuations in currency rates. The wage demands in the intensified inflationary economies of 1973-74 ran directly into conflict with the state's incomes policies of wage controls, transforming strikes, particularly in critical industries, into political struggle, and heightening all aspects of class conflict.

Further complicating the position of capitalists is the new response of labor to the very work process itself. It is not that work in the factory is more unendurable than in the past, although automation has accentuated its robot quality. It is simply that this is a historic period where everywhere in the industrial world, when living standards are beyond the subsistence level, the working class is simply refusing to cooperate with the institutions of exploitation in the work place, be it the factory, the union, or the party. And no one is more acutely aware of this fact than the managing capitalists themselves. While the academic sociologists have for over a decade celebrated or bewailed the alleged existence of a new working class in industrial societies — one drugged by TV, quiescent, and the like — the industrialists face a different reality everywhere. Some corporations, such as ICI, General Electric, and General Foods, have made certain profitable efforts to restructure the work process by giving workers greater leeway in decisions on organization of the job and have reported vastly increased productivity and decline in absenteeism. In various countries, several companies in the auto industry are simultaneously restructuring the assembly line, as with Volvo in Sweden, Fiat in Turin, and GM in California, or are facing strikes against the organization of production itself.

Nevertheless, it is a risky affair and it is costly in the short run. For characteristic is the attitude of the Ford executive who noted, "The production-line technique is the most economic method of producing cars and when you are in competition you just cannot afford to put yourself at an economic disadvantage. But it is arguable that we are reaching the breaking point."[23] It is also risky to tamper with the authoritarian structure inherent in the capitalist organization of work, as it can only underline the parasitic and superfluous role of the management itself. It is in many cases an easier and more familiar path to seek an environment where subsistence living standards or a police state permit the old techniques to be employed, at least for the moment, without question.

Hence we see that the old methods of the advanced industries of accepting the periodic wage increases of the well organized workers and passing the cost on to the consumer in a predictable fashion is, from their point of view, coming to an end. This very loss of predictability, from the inability of the union or the Communist party to control the workers in the work place to the new militant role of the foreign workers, is crucial. In the context of the other conditions in the world economy, it is extremely important in the decision-making of giant corporations.

Another critical dimension of potential social conflict is the workers' response to company bankruptcies and closures. With the congruence of renewed worker militancy and the economic crises inherent in the competitive export market and the search for lower costs, the frequency of worker takeover and occupation of plants may increase. The most publicized and important of these takeovers was that of the Lip watch factory in Besançon, France, because there production continued, and the experience had a widespread impact in France; but in Italy 50 factories have been occupied, one since March 1971 and another for over a year. In Liege, Belgium, workers "took over" an electrical appliance company that had gone bankrupt in 1973. In another French town 90 workers in a shirt factory simply moved to a farm building to continue production on their own. More important, three large French corporations in financial trouble, the truck manufacturer Berliet and two textile firms, collectively employing 67,000 workers, expect Lip-type takeovers if they lay off workers — and are appealing to the government for assistance.[24]

It is not difficult to see the crises brewing in these dynamics: growth based in large part on export industries, and resting in the past on the unstable, war-induced, aggregate demand in the U.S., a fragile international credit structure and the competitive search for lower costs. Politically, everyone recognizes that the working class is no longer a predictable element in the industrial states, both in the nature of its demands and the spontaneous, nonsystematized expression of them. It is this congruence of numerous factors operating simultaneously in world capitalism that is critical. Any one factor discussed in this book in isolation would shrink in significance, but operating concurrently, within the framework of capitalist behavior, they can be seen as a progressive shift forward in the evolution of world capitalism and not merely as a cyclical phenomenon.

## Capitalist Response

The capitalist response to the changing economic environment of the past five years is an active process and the outcome of the simple calculus that defines capitalist behavior everywhere — the pursuit of profit and avoidance of loss. Each move based on that calculus is dynamic because it introduces new conflicts and contradictions into the system to which all must once more respond. This is particularly true of the gigantic corporations which dominate the economies of the industrial states. Their decisions on the questions of production in response to the new elements in the world economy are significant for the future of industrial capitalism.

Export competition, mounting costs, "profitless growth," and losses, are the current challenges among the world's largest corporations. "Why," asked a German business journal in October 1972, "is Volkswagen . . . hovering on the brink of the red, and . . . Opel showing virtually no profit increase?"[25]   It found its answer in the 40 percent wage increase over the previous three years and the fact that foreign cars were claiming 28 percent of the German market during the first six months of 1972.  The change in currency values gave a boost to Renault and Fiat, and Japanese imports were beginning to have an impact.  In January 1973 the president of the largest machine tool firm lamented, "We are pricing ourselves out of world markets. . . . Now we have to think of new ways to control production costs."[26] Such efforts are critical, for 50 percent of the German machine tool production is exported.  In 1972 Krupp was again operating at a loss and KHD had its worst year since World War II — a loss of DM50 million compared to profit of DM12 million in 1971.

In the summer of 1972 Carl Zeiss, after heavy losses due to Japanese and East European competition, closed the last camera plant in West Germany.  The corporation plans to shift to highly specialized optic equipment for the Bonn Defense Ministry.  Rollei had already moved its entire camera production to Singapore not long before.

The developments in VW are indicative of overall trends. Volkswagen is, by far, West Germany's largest corporation, employing one out of every 20 workers, with the share of foreign business in total sales at 69 percent in 1970.  It also accounted for one-third of the $4 billion total German exports to the U.S. in that same year.  Significant therefore for the entire economy, not only of Germany, but the other economies of Europe as well, is the fact that profits shrunk from ". . . well over £100 million to less than £10 million in three years."[27]   And in 1971, German VW production "failed to earn a pfennig."[28]

Although finding a "positive" direction in overall profits in mid-1973, the corporation announced that it expected its American operation to be in the red that year for the first time since it started sales in the U.S. Although the unanticipated 1973 oil crisis gave a temporary boost to American sales, it drastically reduced sales in Europe by 50 percent over the last two months of the year. In part a result of the new currency parities, VW considered, but quickly abandoned, the idea of production in the U.S. itself. For the critical problem is labor costs, costs which necessitate moving to the Third World in order to be competitive in export markets and perhaps in Germany itself. In 1972, after an overhaul of the management, the executives decided that they could not profitably produce the famous "beetle" in Germany at all and planning was underway to transfer more production to an "offshore" facility, namely Brazil. In 1973 VW planned to double its exports from Brazil. It was reported in the business press that the new head of Volkswagen ". . . like his Detroit brethren . . . sees the cheap labor and financial incentives offered by developing nations as the best way to cut production costs."[29] VW has established large and profitable production facilities in Brazil, Mexico, and South Africa, assembly plants in Venezuela and Indonesia, and is preparing to set up other plants in Nigeria and Thailand. In July 1973 the president of VW declared that it would establish "a worldwide trading company, based in Brazil," and from there and other Third World countries it could export to the U.S. and to Europe.[30] In the first half of 1973 German direct foreign investment was greater than in all of 1972.

### Italy

During 1971 and 1972 significant changes were made in the critical Italian industries. After several years of "joint venture," Phillips purchased the failing Ignis, one of the two largest appliance companies, with one-third the Italian market and nearly one-quarter of the European, with the intent of "streamlining" its production — which was understood in the industry, despite denials, to mean closing down factories in Italy or vastly curtailing production there. The second-largest company, Zanussi, was sold shortly thereafter to Telefunken, and Philco sold its Bergamo plant to yet another German company. A curtailment of Italian production was seen in each case as a result of "unruly labor."[31]

Fiat, highly profitable in the period of growth and relatively passive workers, in 1970 saw its profits fall by 60 percent. Now it is reported to be considering marketing the Spanish and Polish Fiats elsewhere in Europe. On overall production Fiat also suffers from "profitless growth." In 1972 sales increased 20 percent but profits remained the same, a return on sales of under 1 percent. Foreign sales dropped 30 to 60 percent at the end of 1973, due to the oil crisis. The corporation applied during the summer of 1972 for production facilities in Brazil, much to the alarm of VW, where it will build a $230 million auto plant in 1973 as well as purchase 40 percent of Alfa Romeo's truck plant. Fiat in this regard is only following a growing trend, as VW and the Detroit "Big Three" decided to expand facilities in Brazil the same year. Ford will produce one-quarter million engines there, mostly for export.

Pirelli, Italy's largest tire company, was operating at only 70 percent capacity at the end of 1972 and losing a large part of its market to Michelin. Its losses for the year ending April 30, 1973, were 26 billion lire, in contrast to a loss of 3.7 billion the previous year. Labor costs increased 75 percent since 1969, making its expenses in Italy 7 percent higher than its German production. It has threatened to lay off 850 Italian workers and transfer more production out of Italy. By June 1972, Montedison, which produces 50 percent of Italian chemicals, announced that it lost $369 million in 1971, and *Business Week* reported in 1972 it had "the biggest loss ever reported by a company anywhere" — $789 million.[32]  Its proposed cure is to close plants and reduce the work force by over 14,000 workers. It closed 14 plants in the fall of 1972 and was challenged by strikes and worker occupation of the buildings before the government asked for a temporary suspension of further closures.

There was by 1972 a trend for Italian corporations to move their funds to Switzerland and their investments abroad. By the end of 1971 plant utilization for the entire Italian economy was 76.4 percent, and it continued at the same rate into 1973. 1971 was the first year since the war with no growth, and production actually declined by 3.5 percent. And in 1972 economic growth was less than 3 percent.

Finally, in 1973 the capital flight due to the economic situation had reached the point where the Italian government introduced a two-tier money market on January 22 and then was forced to float the lira outside the EEC bloc. Such efforts were to little avail, for the capital continued to flow for some time at a rate of more than $250 million a month. At the same time, inflation that the government blamed on rising labor costs threatened any recovery. The exultant early reports of the business press on the economic "miracle" had turned in a few years to complaints of strikes, absenteeism, instability, and sour forebodings on the "sick" and "irreparable" Italian "decadence."[33]

Meanwhile, U.S. industry in Europe is rushing to set up factories in Spain to supply the rest of Europe as the tariffs on Spanish goods into the EEC are progressively lowered. What with the skilled and low-paid Spanish workers, and a fascist regime to guarantee relative "labor peace," "Spain could be the Japan of Europe," according to the eager head of Honeywell in Madrid.[34] One of their executives at a Europe-wide Honeywell meeting underlined that the same machine operator makes $100 per week in Britain, $152 in Germany, and $53 in Spain. According to the director of Armco Steel, the government "can go on providing the roads, harbors, police force and other things needed to make it attractive."[35] Other corporate executives compared Spain of today to Italy in the 1950s in its potential for growth and profit. It is a typically shortsighted analysis, but one on which capitalists just as typically will act.

As the EEC opens progressively to Spanish products, the MNCs are making plans partly to close down plants in

other, more costly, European countries where the workers
are increasingly unpredictable and transfer production to
Spain. The list includes DuPont, ITT, Westinghouse, U.S. Steel,
IBM, and many others, all reacting to the same drives and the
same great incentives. Ford is constructing a plant south of
Valencia to produce 240,000 cars a year by 1977, nearly all
destined for export. A search for a tranquil labor force was
the primary motive for the move. Chrysler, Fiat, Leyland
Motors, and Citroen are also expanding their production in
Spain for the same reason. The EEC proposed a free trade
association for industrial, but not agricultural, goods by
1977. While this is unsatisfactory to the Spanish government, which hoped for full participation in the EEC, it is of
the greatest interest to the foreign industries investing in
Spain.

In Japan as well the situation had changed dramatically
by 1970 due less to worker agitation than to labor shortage
and increasingly high costs. Saburo Okita, president of the
Japan Economic Research Center, testified to a committee
of the U.S. Congress in 1970 that the labor shortage and
rising wages of Japan were reducing its competitiveness in relation to such countries as Taiwan, South Korea, Hong Kong,
and the other Third World countries of the region.[36] The
revaluation of the yen by nearly 40 percent since 1971 has
further stimulated this move to secure lower costs and easier
access to the foreign markets.

A 1971 survey of 800 small Japanese companies revealed
that 100 of them would move overseas in search of cheaper
labor to better produce for export. Discriminations in tariffs
in favor of "developing countries," especially in the U.S., will
accelerate the movement of Japanese investment in Asia,
Africa, and Latin America. As early as 1969 there were 200
Japanese corporations in Latin America, or 21 percent of its
overseas investment. While the larger part was in raw materials, the trend was toward manufacturing as well. Ishikawa-
jima Heavy Industries had built the largest shipyard in
Brazil. And in 1973 Toyota, already producing trucks, was
drawing up plans for a car factory there. By 1973 Brazil had

an estimated total of $600 million in Japanese investment, including electronics, shoes, petrochemicals, and steel.

From Brazil the Japanese will export to the U.S. In 1972 they sent $13 million worth of shoes and the new steel plant in Sao Paulo is intended to supply the U.S. market. What will this vast over-expansion mean at the very time plans are being made to "slow down" the "overheated" American economy and the American steel companies themselves are just pulling out of the red? And the dependence of the steel industry in Japan on exports was heightened during 1972 when it exported 30 percent of production in contrast to 10 percent in 1967.

By the end of March 1973 "hundreds" of Japanese electronics companies were moving to Korea, Singapore, and Malaysia, where wages were one-fifth those of Japan. *Business Week* reported that the entire labor-intensive industry, including the giants, was beginning to move out of Japan.[37] What will this vast over-expansion mean at the very time try do to the Japanese market? We can be sure that this is only the beginning as the drive for lower costs affects the other industries as well. Where will these new offshore companies, with a seemingly unlimited supply of cheap labor, sell their goods?

Although Japan's GNP rose again in 1972 by 11.5 percent, higher consumer spending in the inflationary economy as well as increased building costs accounted for the increase and scarcely masked the serious fissures in the economy. By mid-1973 Japan was tallying up record balance-of-payments deficits, chiefly, like the U.S. in recent years, in the errors and omissions category. Its trade surplus was falling by nearly one-half, and, most critically, the outflow of its foreign investments more than tripled over the previous year. Meanwhile, the government, in order to benefit the Japanese companies who are moving to the Third World in search of lower labor costs, and in a step identical to that of the U.S., lowered its tariffs on goods from the "developing" countries. This decision is expected to increase imports from those countries over the coming year by more than three times —

from $367 million to $1.2 billion. Furthermore, the Japanese ruling society of businessmen, Keidanren, announced that it wanted the Japanese government to direct its "aid" specifically to build the "infrastructure" in those areas chosen by the Japanese private investor.[38]

Another critical motive for Japanese investment overseas is that the islands literally cannot survive further industrial pollution. The Japanese diverted no investment whatever to control the ravages that the rapid industrialization had on the environment, to the extent where pollution today has reached the point of poisoning the very workers and consumers on which the so-called Japanese "miracle" is based. The petrochemical industry, one of the leading polluters, increased output by tenfold between 1960 and 1968, actually doubling between 1965 and 1966. Rather than make the expensive outlays to control pollution, it is less costly to pollute the environment of another people. In Thailand, for example, the Japanese are constructing a petrochemical plant and, in response to the protest of some Thais, Saburo Okita replied, "Developing countries with a per capita income of $1,000 or less can't afford the luxury of worrying about pollution."[39] The necessity to curb this wanton pollution in Japan today will affect the economy in a number of ways. New regulations are forcing the petrochemical industry to make plans for expansion abroad. The cutback of production of certain chemical products necessary to the production of electrical wiring has already created severe shortages and a general slowdown in the construction industry. To meet domestic demand, the Japanese cut back on exports, and these cutbacks are expected to have an injurious effect on certain markets, particularly in Asia. The vulnerability of the Japanese economy to any reduction of supplies became increasingly clear during the last half of 1973. Bankers anticipated that the unexpected shortages would hasten the general business slowdown in prospect in 1974.

There is considerable evidence that the domestic market for Japan's key industries was approaching saturation in 1973 and it will surely decline even more swiftly as manufacturing firms flee to the Third World and as the government, like its capitalist brethren elsewhere, begins to introduce deflationary monetary and fiscal measures. According to the Nomura Research Institute, these measures should begin to have serious effect by the end of 1973 and will make the business environment unfavorable. With a nearly 40 percent increase in the value of the yen, Japanese goods are no longer as competitive in foreign markets and are meeting ever greater barriers in the American and European markets.

In the struggle for markets Japan must simultaneously secure new outlets and retain those that it has developed. The same is true for its supplies of raw materials. The immense economic machine of Japan devours nearly 20 percent of the world's consumption of raw materials, and if projections are realized — and they rarely are — it would be 30 percent by 1980. At present Japan is the world's leading importer of raw materials, which, at latest figures, made up 60 percent of its imports. Petroleum accounted for 15 percent of those imports. The Japanese are prospecting in Africa and Latin and North America in an effort to find diverse sources for the materials they need, particularly oil. When the Arab oil states, the source of 85 percent of its petroleum in 1970, introduced their embargo and there was evidence that the major oil companies which control the vast majority of its imports were redirecting fuel to others, a period of panic was followed by a furtive Japanese political shift toward the Arab states, coupled with increased promises of economic aid. The increased costs appeared to have more serious implications to the balance-of-payments, inflation, and hence Japan's need to take political steps to increase the competitiveness of its exports.

In the East Asia-Pacific zone Japan cannot gain much at the expense of the other industrial states, for it already dominates both the imports and exports of the area, although they comprise only a fraction of Japan's total needs. Although in 1960 one-third of Japanese exports and 20 percent of its imports were with the Asia-Pacific zone, the Japanese emphasis on the region has declined consistently while the importance of Japan for the region has grown enormously. By 1971 only 25 percent of Japanese exports and 15 percent of its imports were linked to the region, yet Japan is by far the major supplier and most important customer. For instance, in 1973 Japan bought 73 percent of Indonesia's oil production, which accounted for only 17 percent of Japan's oil imports. As Japan's trade surplus continued to decline in 1973, Keidanren urged greater effort by the government to stimulate exports in order to pay for essential imports. It called on the Japanese corporations to continue to press for lower costs and higher productivity.

"Never before have I felt so keenly the difficult state of affairs that is before us," worried the president of Keidanren in the fall of 1973. "Many and various needs of the nation, which so far have been hidden, have surfaced at once."[40] Projections of the Japanese experience over the past two decades into the future, a fashion among academics and journalists, is irrelevant, for it ignores the exceptional context of its remarkable growth — an economic boom that was largely comprised of factors that either have disappeared or are not likely to repeat themselves.

### Capitalist "Planning"

Superimposed on the self-generating behavior of the private corporations, and able sharply to aggravate its consequences, is the closest thing to capitalist "planning" — a conscious manipulation of government fiscal and monetary policies to determine the general environment that will assist the operations of private interests. Confronted by insoluble dilemmas brought on by the very operation of the system they are trying to preserve, the various capitalist states attempt to shape an environment conducive to its profitable operation and stability. Attempts to control inflation and recessions, to create regional markets such as the EEC, or to establish rules for a trading and monetary system, inevitably create new contradictions and conflict. Basically, all in positions of power in capitalist states are bound, to one degree or another, by orthodox precepts of policy, whether they proclaim adherence to Keynesiansim, Social Democracy, or the "free market." And naturally they will always, as far as politically possible, make the working class pay for their efforts to balance budgets, international payments, and to control inflation. All of the supranational organizations, such as the EEC, OECD, World Bank, IMF, BIS, Development Banks, and the like, are made up of the guardians of this faith, firmly convinced in the correctness of their policies. They are dedicated to stability and balance in economies, currencies, budgets, payments in an intrinsically chaotic world system, and can find economic stability momentarily in stagnation, which in turn generates new conflict and contradictions. How far "disciplinary" deflationary measures are allowed to operate depends on the overall power or dependence of individual nations. At the end of World War II, when the U.S. could direct the European and Japanese economies, it demanded an iron rigor in implementing these policies with no regard for the internal political consequences. And as discussed in *The Limits of Power,* this led to serious results for which they had to compensate with other, usually military measures, in the sense of direct support to the economy through expenditures for war.

### Capitalist "Planning": The British Case

A prime example of these attempts to shape the economic environment is the incredible efforts of both the British Conservative and Labour Governments to use deflationary economic policies to deal with economic crises — namely speculative runs on the pound — that had little to do with the actual condition of the British economy, even from a conservative point of view. Nevertheless, they repeatedly went through the motions of reducing economic activity and raising unemployment in order to "curtail demand" for imports, whenever their reserves were drained through speculation. This came to be known as their "stop-go" economy.

These traditional responses were not solely the decisions of the British government, since there was considerable pressure by Britain's international creditors. Four times between 1964 and 1968 the European central banks, through the BIS (to the probable sum of $4.8 billion) and the IMF, came to the assistance of Britain's leaking reserves on the condition that the government seek a structural solution through the means of orthodox fiscal and monetary policies. It did not matter that such measures were irrelevant to the nature of the problem. The currency drawing rights or loans were to save the British reserves and guarantee the convertibility of the pound. Deflationary policies are a reactionary cure for a trade imbalance but the critical factor in the British crises was the massive capital outflow into other currencies. Britain did have a trade deficit throughout the 1960s but this is a "traditional" feature of British payments. The so-called "invisibles" are always in surplus but were less able to cover the trade deficit in part because of an increase in Britain's military expenditures overseas by four times throughout the 1960s and tax provisions encouraged foreign investment. Its crises were triggered by speculative attacks on the pound as well as massive shifts into Eurodollars during their periods of high interest — 1966 and 1969.

There was a rush on the pound and a sterling crisis following the BLP's electoral victory in November 1964. During the next crisis in September 1965 the IMF and BIS elicited a vague promise on an incomes policy. After the sterling crisis of July 1966 the Labour government put the economy through the "discipline" of deflationary measures directly aimed at the working class to handle the balance-of-payments drain, caused by speculators with the pound. Finally, in December 1967, after a long deflationary struggle that failed entirely to stop a run on the pound, the government devalued. The advice of the BIS and IMF on these occasions was to curtail consumption and increase unemployment and incentives for investment. The IMF was able to secure a "Letter of Intent" to pursue such policies, similar to those it extracts from the Third World nations. And both the Labour and Conservative governments took all the measures to squeeze a surplus from the working class through unemployment and reduced consumption to compensate for the speculation with the national currency. But the various governments naturally failed altogether to restore the confidence of the bourgeoisie in either the currency or the economy, and the speculation continued. Such a discussion is not meant to imply that speculation is the only problem with the British economy or that it may not reflect other dilemmas leading to a lack of confidence. It is nevertheless true that speculation over the 1960s, whose origin may have been as peripheral as a differential of interest rates, led to each crisis, and the government responded with measures aimed at the living conditions of the workers, creating greater crises for the future.

For several years prior to British entry into the EEC the government had been introducing additional measures to "discipline" the country for the sharpened competitive struggle. The primary question was the British worker, a real problem of competitive cost accounting that had disturbed the British capitalists for some time. The incomes policy, and perhaps anti-strike laws, were regarded as essential to enter the Community with anything but competitive disadvantages.

In March 1972 London modified its controls on direct investment outflow and British capital scurried at record speed to flee what appeared to them a sinking domestic economy and buy everything they could on the continent, especially in France. This caused a transitional boom in the European stock markets, but for the British economy this outflow of capital had other implications. By summer the government was forced to float the pound, maintaining the float after entry into the EEC because of the weakness of British economic confidence. Toward the end of 1973 pressures were again mounting both internally and from international creditors to introduce an austerity program once more.

The British guarantee of deposits at a fixed rate to foreign depositors established in 1968 with the backing of the IMF, and renewed for two years in 1971, expired in September 1973. To avoid a new monetary crisis, the IMF again guaranteed the pound for another six months. The sterling area countries have roughly $5 billion deposited as reserves in London and without the international guarantee of the pound at $2.42 the deposits may have been withdrawn precipitously. Britain does not have the liquid capital to meet these obligations. The U.S. is in an even worse position but because of its international position of power it plays a different role *vis-à-vis* its creditors. The IMF has new leverage on British economic policy. In this regard they are particularly anxious about the possibility of new labor strikes that would further undermine the British balance of trade and payments.[41]

The British government doggedly pursued its traditional anti-inflationary program of reducing the spending power of the working class, cutting government spending in those areas of health and education to further decrease public demand, and raising the interest rate to a record 13 percent. Nevertheless, inflation continued at over 10.3 percent, the pound dropped to its lowest point, and the trade deficit in October 1973 — before the rise in oil prices — was the highest in British history. The government then chose to have its confrontation with the coal miners, who refused to accept the arbitrary decree of a limit on wage demands. By the end of the year what was an economic crisis had manifestly evolved into an intense social crisis of class conflict. The political terrain had shifted markedly since the British government had earlier introduced its traditional deflationary policies.

### The EEC

The supranational trade organizations, such as the EEC, scarcely provide an answer to the mounting crisis of Western capitalism. On the contrary, the EEC is developing into a focal point of conflict both with the U.S. and with Japan, and it has produced innumerable points of internal tension.

The Treaty of Rome, which in 1958 organized the European Economic Community, embodied all the principles of capitalist internationalism which the political leaders of Europe had deliberated at length since the war. Conservative in

its very essence, it committed the member nations to orthodox economic principles of balanced economies that earned it
the designation of the "Bankers' Europe." The emphasis on
trade and payments balance among members, and the pressure on any member running a trade deficit to apply deflationary policies to reduce imports by reducing employment,
in principle was to harmonize Europe's economic and monetary policies. The other goal was to "rationalize" the industrial sector by allowing the industrial giants to sweep aside
small, supposedly less efficient, firms. Nowhere is there a
reference, even rhetorically, to maintaining full employment
— only provisions for the mobility of labor. In agriculture,
on the other hand, protection of the small farmer was a key-
stone of the treaty primarily because large-scale agriculture
has no political power. Progressively over the subsequent
12 years the EEC eliminated all tariffs between the member
states and set up a common wall of a single tariff to protect
the Community from the rest of the world. Eventually, the
EEC was to create a single currency for the entire Community, in concert with a single monetary policy. By 1973 all
that had in fact evolved was a customs union with a single
agricultural policy, the latter being the symbol of the EEC
itself.

In addition to the nine full members of the EEC, the
Community has negotiated special ties with the southern
European and Mediterranean states, 18 African, and even a
few Latin American governments, for raw materials and markets to provide mutually advantageous and discriminatory
trade relationships.

The potential strength of the EEC is great indeed. United
it would be the most powerful economic unit in the world and
its efforts to shape future monetary and trade structures could
be decisive. But this potential giant is only an abstraction.
The European states remain capitalist and are subject to the
same crises and contradictions. There are many decisive elements which will probably break the whole effort on the shoals
of protectionism if recessionary forces intensify.

To cite only a few cases of deep divisions, in May 1971

the Germans floated their currency without a word of consultation with their European partners, intending *de facto* to force the other EEC members to do the same. France refused to yield. Finally, on the most sensitive issue in the EEC — agriculture — the Italian government imported U.S. grain at the end of December 1971 for sale in the Italian market at less than the EEC members' products. The EEC warned the Italian government, without success, that it must grant the low-bidding German electrical company contracts which domestic political pressure insisted go to the higher bidding Italian. It also tried unsuccessfully to force Italy to curtail advantages of the government corporations.

All of the monetary negotiations were intensely disputatious, causing conflict primarily between Germany and France. Finally, the joint float in the spring of 1973 was an emergency accord, with France yielding essentially to the American demands. Three of the nine members, Britain, Italy and Ireland, remained outside out of fear that the capital outflow at a pegged rate with the stronger mark and franc would overwhelm their national treasuries.[42]  If any force prods Europe into real unity it will be their essential defensive reaction to the U.S.  But while the Europeans share a growing incredulity toward both U.S. policy and style, they hardly have greater regard for each other. The efforts to achieve unity in times of general prosperity will go to shambles in times of economic crisis. The late 1973 scramble to secure special advantages in the Middle East to guarantee oil supplies, accompanied by monetary shifts that foretold the race for competitive devaluations and conflict between Britain and Germany on a regional development fund, all accentuated the latent rivalry that exists between these capitalist nations simultaneously suffering the same symptoms of the same malaise.

The U.S. had been a prime mover of European unity from the end of the war until the creation of the EEC in 1958. And although it had abstractly considered the possibility that the organization might in the future pose a potential competitive threat, the more pressing existence of a dollar gap at the time made it seem remote indeed. And all the underlying concepts of rationalizing European capitalism to make it competitive enough to earn dollars without aid had been theirs since the inception of the Marshall Plan.

Preoccupied with the war in Vietnam, which provided sufficient demand for goods and services, U.S. industry did not worry excessively over the competition from imports or in the export markets. Whenever there is sufficient demand domestically, there is little motivation for an American businessman to push for an export market; but according to one banker, "When that base shrinks during a recession he tries to supplement it with foreign sales. . .," but by then it is generally too late.[43] They were busy, in any case, meeting the demand abroad by setting up new factories and expanding overseas facilities. For the largest American corporations the establishment of the EEC was distinctly in their own interest for it eliminated the need to duplicate plant and expanded the market for sales and hence profits. As the country with the most American investment in Europe, Britain's entry was an even greater boon for the American international corporations. Nevertheless, even in exports the U.S. had a growth of at least 161 percent between 1958 and 1969 to the EEC nations.

In agriculture there was always conflict, from the "chicken war" of the early 1960s to the intensely hostile encounters at the present time. With the recent accumulation of economic crises and the pressures generated by the recession of 1969-71, many in Washington have come to view the EEC as directly contrary to America's national interest, and the pressure is preeminently from agricultural interests which cannot profitably participate in the economic unity and have lost 40 percent of their sales to Western Europe in four years. With British entry, another $500 million was endangered. In 1972, Secretary of Commerce Peterson decried the "tragic" evolution of European agricultural policies.[44] The recent wheat sales to the U.S.S.R. and the promised future market there, plus shortages of many commodities, have temporarily relieved the intensity of the pressure. But the 1973 boycott on soybean exports stimulated the EEC to subsidize production in France.

Most infuriating to the U.S. is not the EEC itself but the preferential trade pacts with the Mediterranean countries, Africa, Northern Europe, and now parts of the British Commonwealth. "You look around," a U.S. official complained,"and they're fencing off a hell of a large part of the world."[45]  Supposedly, they are looking for a new "political" relationship with Latin America, and this will be particularly true of Argentina under Perón.  One British official gloated that in a few years the EEC would have the Communist market "sewed up."[46]  By 1973 American and European officials recognized that they were on a collision course, with relations as bad as at any time since World War II.  From steel to shoes, and aggravated immeasurably by the oil crisis of winter 1973, conflict is now endemic, and as the struggle for markets intensifies and protectionism follows, hostility will only grow.  It is a struggle for materials in times of full production and a struggle for markets during stagnation and recession.

## Conclusion

The industrial economies are again being drawn into the whirlpool of contradictions and conflict as they try simultaneously to control inflation, protect their currencies, maintain or secure a trade advantage and a growing economy.  And by 1973 their moves were synchronized for the first time since World War II.  The real underlying condition of the industrial economies is perilous at best, and their imposing physical plant and production statistics merely hide the fundamental fact that they all still rest on the same fragile and irrational social system.

As the competitive struggle for a narrowing market intensifies, as cost advantages disappear, industries throughout the industrial capitalist nations are moving to the Third World, to Spain, or to Eastern Europe in order to compensate and compete.  But their predicament is heightened in that they are all looking simultaneously for the same solution.  World productive capacity in both industrial and consumer goods has greatly expanded at the very time that monetary and fiscal policies are increasingly restricting economic activity everywhere. And the very move out of the industrial nations, coupled with the other monetary and trade struggles, can only reduce employment, weaken these nations' own market for their new capacity, and accentuate the social and political conflict they seek to avoid.

The congruence of all these forces, contradictions, and crisis-inducing responses from the capitalists and their governments is leading to a situation in the industrial world that is one of potentially explosive economic, political, and social conflict.

### CHAPTER FIVE

# THE THIRD WORLD AND THE CRISIS IN
# WORLD CAPITALISM

There is a danger in categories that can ensnare even the most wary. This is particularly true in discussions of the so-called Third World, the pre-industrial states which encompass such vast geographic, historic, and cultural diversity and whose people account for more than half of the world's population. Yet, the crucial point here is that despite the cultural and historic variations, one economic system girdles the globe and subjects all of these diverse states that possess subsistence-wage workers and raw materials to ruthless exploitation and violent repression. It is this impact of imperialism that permits such categorization of otherwise incomparable areas of the world into arbitrary terms such as "Third World."

The past two decades have seen much violence and increased misery but little basic change in the fundamental dependence of the Third World on the capitalist industrial states, and this integration, by definition, precludes changes in the structural base of imperialism which permeates the economies of most of the preindustrial nations. In 1950, with the exception of China and North Korea, all of Africa, Asia, and Latin America fell into the category of the Third World subject to the capitalist industrial states of the West. More than two decades later, only North Vietnam and Cuba had moved decisively out of this orbit.

Hundreds of specialized and general studies, reflecting a multiplicity of viewpoints, have been written dealing with the problems of the "Third World," especially since the 1950s. As such questions encompass a vast magnitude of complex issues, suffice it to say that in one chapter of this short volume I can only raise certain questions and point to a few trends in the relationship of the Third World to the present crisis of world capitalism. Much of the material has already been ably discussed by others, and in some cases I merely bring earlier discussions up-to-date. Nevertheless, it is impossible to comprehend the global nature of the problems of this study without examining the broad contours of the interrelationship of the preindustrial areas of the world to the advanced capitalist states.

Obviously, in the vast areas comprising, in the oversimplified lexicon of academics, the "Third World," the regions and governments differ radically from one another. But they do share certain characteristics which permit one to examine the economic impact of the Western capitalism on the preindustrial states as a whole. The most crucial common points of these predominantly agrarian economies are their reliance on the foreign market for primary products, a low industrial base, a more inequitable distribution of income, vast unemployment and low-paid, unskilled workers outside of the production process, subsistence mass living standards at best, and low per capita production and income which mean a low base for investment and industrialization. And, of course, the vast majority have only recently emerged from political subservience to an industrial power and still remain under continued economic domination by foreign capital. Many of the structural problems of the Third World such as famine, monoculture, erosion, and land tenure were the heritage of that colonialism. The social systems range from tribal, feudal, mercantile, compradore, bourgeois national capitalist, mixed economies, or centrally planned economies. I will not discuss the latter in this chapter, as they do not relate to the Western capitalist states, except to point out that many of the socalled endemic problems of unemployment, famine, and overpopulation no longer afflict them. They are either large enough, as China, to carry out their own development independently or, like Cuba and the DRV, integrally linked to the centrally planned economies of Eastern Europe or China.

## The "Infrastructure" of Development

With the process of decolonization and, principally, the boom in raw materials exploration during the early 1950s, the international financial organizations began to infiltrate the Third World to replace the colonial regimes and to help build the infrastructure for private investment. Economists, no less than generals and jailers, have their role to play in this process. And there is a capitalist consensus, so axiomatic as to be rarely formulated as a question, that an infrastructure means more than transportation, ports, power supplies, and the like; it also means an economic environment, a framework of fiscal and monetary policies conducive to "development" along essentially unquestioned and preconceived capitalist paths — assumptions which are, more than incidentally, harmonious with the needs of private investment. There is also a parallel need for political receptivity and a security infrastructure. The international experts and bankers were to guide the new nations of the Third World in the principles of macro-economic government management and together with infusions of loans of hard currencies for foreign exchange were to achieve, through steady economic growth, "development."

As we have seen elsewhere, there is an intertwined dynamic process in capitalism of the private pursuit of profit continuously and singlemindedly thrusting outward, creating crises and contradictions in the process. Simultaneously academic economists and bankers in governments, by manipulating levers of national economic policies according to given precepts, try to establish the economic environment within which this dynamic can take place. Intending to achieve one aim, they invariably create new and unanticipated crises.

Imposed, therefore, on the vast preindustrial regions of the world was a whole paraphernalia of orthodox economic precepts of balanced budgets, stable currencies, payments balances, and a series of wholly irrelevant concepts of "growth"

drawn from narrow reflections on the economic histories of
the industrial states themselves. The development experts operate through new national regimes which had, for the most part,
made their peace with their old colonial masters and are serving
in a compradore capacity or who represent old feudal landlord
interests.

In addition, over the past two decades an entire ideology
of "foreign aid" was constructed which purported that an infusion of money from the "rich countries" to the "poor countries"
would transform the latter areas. In the U.S. the ideology went
from the unsophisticated response of the public and Congress
linking "aid" either to charity or military security to the more
elaborate theories of academics and policymakers that there are
"keys," such as the infusion of foreign exchange, that would
begin the process of development and thereby lead to the "take-
off points" of self-sustained growth. As often as not, it was
simply a bribe to a country's ruling clique for favors expected.
Some economists have uncritically linked economic growth to
the infusions of "aid" as if it were the sole causal ingredient,
ignoring the other determining factors of expanded demand and
markets in the industrial world due to often far more influential,
but unplanned, political factors — primarily war.[1] With the
multiplicity of new nations, an army of international bureaucrats in the IMF and World Bank grant loans, then install
themselves to ascertain how they are administered, propose
the standards of rigorous monetary and fiscal orthodoxy,
and often supervise the local budget.

Over the 1950s and 1960s this dynamic of loans, development advice, and fiscal and monetary manipulations through
the leverage of loans interacted with private investments to
accentuate the crises endemic in various Third World areas
and create even greater misery for the masses of the population.
Unemployment, which the economic strategists now concede to
be the number one problem in the Third World, by the standards
that unemployment is determined in the industrial states, on
the average grew to 30 percent in 1972. Hunger, despite and in
part because of the "Green Revolution," has increased, distribution of income made more inequitable, public and private

debt soared, and the number of landless agricultural laborers grew enormously.

## The Land Problem

Land in the agricultural Third World represents the most ancient legacy of social conflict, stagnation, economic subsistence, and exploitation. The struggle for land is the epic story that has provided the revolutionary force, but not the ideology, to national struggles in the Third World. It is the peasant's ages-old agrarian grievances against the landlord-moneylender which is the foundation of revolutionary national liberation movements. And while land remains the vital question for the masses in most agrarian areas, the last two "development decades" have introduced some significant new factors which have compounded, and in some ways changed structurally, the situation.

As capital in many nations has been made artificially cheap through exchange manipulations, credits, and the like, the large and medium landowners in Asia, Latin America, and elsewhere have been able to buy tractors more readily, as one American government expert pointed out, than the farmer in Iowa.[2] This mechanization has made labor an "inconvenient" factor on the land and has driven many workers to the urban areas. No less significant has been the great deception of the "Green Revolution" within the existing socio-economic structure and its distribution system. Erich Jacoby has authoritatively analyzed the whole process in his *Man and Land,* and I can only note here that the contradictions of agricultural commodity production within the capitalist framework can be vividly comprehended by this example of the introduction of the "miracle rice." With literally millions starving in Asia every year the question of surplus rice production and U.S. dumping of its own surplus in the 1960s led such traditional export countries as Thailand and Burma to predict "long term" depression. In Thailand rice prices fell from $155 per ton in December 1969 to $92 a ton in the same month of 1971. Both India and Japan, earlier rice importers, declared a surplus in January 1972, and Japan in 1970 adopted the American policy of paying farmers not to produce, and began large-scale exports and conversion of rice to fodder. The U.S. government, meanwhile, sold American rice at less on long-term credit. This was no benefit to the hungry, of course, since it was sold through the traditional distribution system; it merely further undermined the peasant's income. Yet even with the "Green Revolution," agricultural production in the Third World increased only 2 percent in 1971 compared to 3 percent for the global total, and food production lagged behind nonfood commodity agriculture.

Most important, the "abundance" of rice along with the mechanization of production has forced peasants into the cities, swelling the already immense ranks of the urban unemployed. The urban growth rate averages 5 percent a year, one-half due to the birth rate and the other half to migration. For example, Lagos grew from 250,000 in 1950 to 1.5 million in 1970; Seoul, from 2.5 to 5 million; Bangkok, from 1 to 3 million, and Bogotá from 650,000 to 2.5 million over the same years. This process simply accelerates the demographic shift already under way everywhere in the Third World, an evolution very different from previous historical transformations from agricultural to industrial societies.[3]

The mechanization of agriculture has also further encouraged the utilization of new land for monoculture plantations geared to export, encroaching on the peasants' land and increasing the need of many areas, once self-sufficient, to import food — as in the Philippines. This monoculture, of course, was one of the most destructive legacies of colonialism and in good part accounted for the famine and destitution in India under the British. The fluctuations of price in these primary agricultural products affects, first, the working minority, and then the profits of the corporations or land-owners. Eventually a crisis in government reserves leads to policies that affect other sectors of the working population, but the majority in many areas of the Third World are already outside the market economy.

### Unemployment

Taking the aggregate of the Third World, in 1972 30 percent

of the population was unemployed by traditional standards. In
Latin America the figure was 26 percent in 1960, and according
to the Food and Agriculture Organization (FAO) has been
"rising steadily since."[4]   Meanwhile, the economies in Latin
America have had an overall growth rate averaging 5-7 percent a year; in Brazil it was 11 percent in 1971. But the
urban population is growing more than  twice as fast as
urban jobs.  Furthermore, the projection is that the number of
workers entering the labor force due only to natural causes during the 1970s will be 50 percent more than in the 1960s. In
most Asian countries 40 to 50 percent of the population is under
14 years of age and the U.N. has estimated Asia will need 173
million new jobs during the 1970s to meet the population growth
alone.

The literal unemployment figures, which can only be very
approximate at best, barely reveal the magnitude of the situation. The vast majority of the "displaced peasants," as Erich
Jacoby cogently defined them, eke out a below-subsistence sur-
vival outside of the commodity production process altogether
by working some 70 to 80 hours a week for the equivalent of
$2 to $3 shining shoes, selling pencils, and similar marginal
services. An economist for the Organization of American
States estimated that in Latin America two-thirds of the
entire *working* labor force is engaged in nonproductive activity. In many areas the unemployed among the university
graduates is no less high. In Pakistan, for example, it ranges
from 24 to 52 percent. This not uncommon level adds its own
social dynamic to the situation. What is more, there is absolutely
no hope for employment for millions within the prevailing economic system.

All "development" policies of the past two decades encouraged capital-intensive industrialization and discouraged
agriculture — making capital relatively cheap with a distorted
price structure, exchange rates, and the like. Great emphasis
was placed on the producer goods industry in the early stages.
Heavy industry even today employs 20 to 40 percent of the total
manufacturing employees in most Asian countries. More recently
there has been a shift in direction with the influx of private capi-

tal in search of labor for the manufacture of many consumer goods. But for this production the multinational corporations have exported their used machinery, equipment that is already highly capital intensive and could never absorb sufficient labor to redress existing unemployment.

These facts are now acknowledged with some trepidation even by the economic "planners" in the industrial states. They view the unemployment as ". . . a time bomb ticking away . . . idle hands reaching out to tear down the systems" in the "politically explosive cities [that] will be a potential of political upheaval everywhere."[5]   These "experts" claim they ignored the problem during the 1950s and 1960s because they believed "development" would eliminate unemployment. It was a shock to acknowledge in 1970 that "growth" had merely aggravated it. That unemployment is now taken very seriously indeed is evidenced by the World Bank's much quoted and discussed Pearson Commission report, as well as the President's Committee on Development headed by Rudolph Peterson, the president of the Bank of America.

As is now well known, the Pearson report, following the lead of the Bank's president, Robert McNamara, subjected its data to a Malthusian analysis and advocated stern measures of population control, implying that future financial assistance should somehow be contingent on a government's undertaking birth control projects among the population. "Aid-givers cannot be indifferent to whether population problems receive the attention they require."[6]   Yet the development experts recognize that population control is a long-term solution that can hardly affect the next 10 to 20 years. For this period they can only raise dire warnings and advocate more labor-intensive investments, increased government grants as opposed to loans from "rich" countries, dearer capital to discourage mechanization, and cheaper labor. They issue warnings that trade unions and minimum wages are luxuries aggravating the problem of unemployment by encouraging investment in machinery. Many official development economists and planners hold up South Korea, Taiwan, and Indonesia as the models for economic and social organization of the Third World, and some ignore, even within the context of their political preferences, that two of these nations were among the largest recipients of U.S. funds, providing some $5 billion in grants alone to Taiwan between 1962 and 1972 and $11.2 billion to South Korea over the same period. Other Third World nations, of course, cannot readily count on sums of this magnitude no matter how hard they might try to emulate the political characteristics of these "models."

Pointing to South Korea, Taiwan, and Indonesia as criteria, of course, undermines every other pious sentiment in the traditional studies and reveals precisely what type of economic environment such agencies and authors desire for the Third World. South Korea, for example, is a paragon of the crassest exploitation, corruption, and social disintegration. It is a brutal dictatorial regime whose largest city is one vast slum, where the population is growing by 1,000 persons a day due to the even inferior conditions in the countryside, and whose urban unemployment hovers at roughly 30 percent. It has, however, excelled in providing cheap labor for the numerous American and Japanese manufacturing industries established in the country. Indonesia's "development" rests on the graves of up to 1 million people from the systematic massacres of 1965-66 and the continued liquidations and concentration camps since that time.[7]

## The Debt Problem

Over the two postwar decades, as is now well known, debt and debt servicing became one of the most crucial problems that the Third World governments faced within the capitalist system. Aggregate government-guaranteed external debts were over $60 billion in 1972, up from $21.5 billion in 1961, and climbing at an annual rate of 14 percent a year. The debt service payments — payments of interest and principal — grew at 17 percent a year and at present are over $5 billion per year for the public debt alone — and climbing twice as fast as export earnings. One-third of that burden is for Latin America, one-third for Asia, and a sixth for Africa — largely concentrated in Ghana. Simply meeting these debts took roughly one-tenth of the Third World's export income. For Latin America as a whole, debt service took 17 percent of all export earnings, and in some countries, well over 25 percent. In 1967, Ghana's external debt service obligations were equivalent to 50 percent of its export income. Perpetuating the trap, 75 percent of all new loans, as an overall average, are made to meet the debt service of old loans; for Latin America, it is 87 percent, for East Asia, 52 percent.[8]

In this context, and given the Third World's politically weak position, its creditors are able to exert considerable "leverage" on the internal economic affairs of the borrowing states. It should also be remembered that the ruling classes of most of these countries are in fundamental agreement with the overall framework of the economic precepts of world capitalism, and in some cases are merely venal gangsters intent on their own enrichment, scarcely with any national pretensions, and content to leave the country to the management of international "experts."

### The IMF and World Bank

The international financial organizations — the IMF, the World Bank, the regional development banks, the OECD Committee on Development, and the like — play a direct role in trying to influence the internal economic policies of the small states to whom they loan funds — precisely as the U.S. applied pressure for definite conservative financial policies in Europe during the Marshall Plan, and in Japan during the occupation, or as the EEC and the BIS try to coordinate the economic policies of their members. The IMF and the World Bank have been more successful in forcing conformity to their views in the Third World because of the overwhelming indebtedness and political weakness of the countries involved.

While the Americans dominate these two organizations, their policies are not exclusively Washington's positions. All bankers are disposed toward deflationary policies, and the purpose of the IMF is to maintain stable values of currencies, while the Bank raises money in the capital market and loans to governments on stiff commercial terms for 10 to 25 years. Both thereby profess an overriding interest in conservative management of fiscal and monetary policies. They also emit the aura of expertise and tutelage as if such fundamental, basically political, decisions as are involved in economic policy were merely questions of technical competence.

As one of the senior advisers of the IMF reflected, "One of the most important activities of the Fund . . . has been to make periodic reviews with members of their economic and financial policies.. . . . it has urged members to formulate annual financial programs designed to achieve financial balance in the economy." "Discussions between the Fund staff and the authorities allow an informal but effective examination of national policies . . . ." During these "discussions" — and the amount of compulsion reflects the power and indebtedness of the country concerned — the Fund staff emphasizes the "sound management of the balance of payments," warns against "excessive generation of credit, especially to the public sector," and "requires a reconsideration . . . of government expenditures — in particular whether some of the less essential . . . can be pruned."[9]

Even more arrogantly, another senior IMF official has described the Fund's activities in the Third World. A staff team of three to four economists in Washington prepares a brief on a country and then discusses it with the government, "usually" in its own capital. In the five years between 1967 and 1972, the IMF dispatched 260 "experts" to 67 countries.

> The discussions are confidential and frank. . . . Naturally national leaders are more preoccupied with the domestic, social, and political problems that policy adjustments may create . . . . On the other hand members of the Fund . . . have been exposed to similar problems by other members and can often . . . strengthen their determination to start on a new path. . . . The staff has a unique opportunity to assist members in their policy formulation and in making innovations of an institutional or policy character.[10]

Their aim is to assure convertibility to allow for the free flow of capital to create confidence in a nation's currency and improve its payments position and price stability. This, of course, has direct implications for foreign investment.

The IMF is able to provide liquidity at a particular juncture of crisis in a government's foreign reserves. In the decade 1962-72, Fund members drew $3.6 billion. In receiving drawing rights of a hard currency, the recipient government writes a "Letter of Intent" declaring its agreement to pursue deflationary policies despite the political repercussions. When the accumulation of debt and debt-service leads a nation to near or actual default, the IMF intervenes and subjects the borrower government to the "surveillance of aid consortia" whereby the creditors multilaterally reschedule the debts and actively force new economic policies on the debtor state. During the two decades after 1950 the Fund introduced many stabilization and surveillance programs throughout the Third World. These have requently followed the political overthrow of a reformist government by a military dictatorship, as in Brazil, Indonesia, and Chile.

The case of Indonesia is an illuminating example of such surveillance. After a prolonged war with the Dutch that only really terminated in 1954 insofar as Indonesian control of the economy was concerned, the government made some rapid strides in general education, construction of railways, electricity, roads and shipping, and training the civil service, maintained an involved system of foreign exchange controls, and introduced subsidies for such essentials as rice, fuel, public transport, and utilities to maintain and raise the living standard. Sukarno incurred a massive foreign debt of $2 billion, one-half to Eastern Europe, to carry out these projects, and although there was considerable corruption and waste of resources, that was scarcely what aroused the hostility of the western capitalists. Rather it was that Sukarno's corruption was not open to their interests, the uses of aid, the default on loans, and, finally and most critically, the nationalization of U.S. investments in 1964-65.

After the "political upheaval" in the fall of 1965 — a bloody organized repression that killed hundreds of thousands over several months — a new government, under the guidance of the aid consortia, predominantly the U.S. and Japan, through the IMF, set about to revamp the economy — after the new government returned the nationalized property to the former owners. The aim of the IMF was a stabilization program to balance the government budget, give strength to the national currency, and eliminate the multiple exchange rates, thereby creating a stable and attractive climate for international investment. Measures taken had to be "unpopular" and the IMF official congratulated the new government for its "courageous decisions" to lower living standards by eliminating all subsidies on the necessities of the working people — kerosene, rice, public transport, and utilities — to allow the market to operate, while at the same time raising incentives to investment.[1]

Elsewhere, as well, the consistent pattern of the international financial organizations is to keep living standards low and prepare the infrastructure of a pool of subsistence wage workers for the multinational industries in search of cheap labor to manufacture for export. In 1969, 15 countries in the Third World were under the surveillance of aid consortia, and many more are expected during the 1970s as defaults become unavoidable.

The International Development Association (IDA), the so-called "soft loan" affiliate of the World Bank, has the same policies, procedures, and staff but obtains its funds from governments and extends credit, at virtually no interest and up to 50 years, to only the "poorest" nations that have exhausted their credit-worthiness. Even then it will assist only those governments "avoiding inflationary policies."[12]

By and large, the World Bank's loans were project-oriented and capital-intensive. There has been a bias against agriculture in general, but when funds were allocated for such purposes they were generally for mechanization. Here output was the criterion and the international institutions conveniently believed that land reform would reduce output. In 1972, following the recommendations of the Pearson Commission, the Bank sought to shift its emphasis from the urban areas and industrial development, and loans to agriculture surpassed loans to other sectors for the first time. At the annual meeting of the World Bank and IMF in 1973, Bank President Robert McNamara called on the industrial states to increase their "aid" through the IDA and to concentrate on the productivity of small-scale agriculture for "solving the problems of absolute poverty in the rural areas." The new emphasis was to be "action . . . which will directly benefit the poorest." These he described as people who have "a condition of life so limited as to prevent realization of the potential of the genes with which one is born."[13] Coming from a man who tried to bomb one small, but indomitable Third World country back to the stone age, an ample measure of skepticism is more than warranted.

In theory the new goal was a major reversal of the Bank's previous emphasis on mechanization of large-scale agriculture in those rare instances when it allocated any loans to the agriculture sector. But at the same time that McNamara called for projects to help the rural poor, the Bank rejected a proposal for rural electrification in Nigeria because its rate of return was not as high as the 15 percent for power projects destined for the urban industrial areas of that nation. So even with new emphasis on the agricultural sector such calculations have been, are, and will continue to be the basis for World Bank loans.

There has also been a complementary relationship between the loans of the international banking institutions and foreign private investment. Raymond Vernon's massive study of the multinational corporations concluded that fully one-fifth to one-quarter of all private investment in the Third World is "directly related" to those loans.[14]

Nevertheless, the World Bank and IMF provided only a small sector of the publicly guaranteed loans contracted by the vast majority of Third World governments. Far more important quantitatively was the profusion of what is termed "suppliers' credits," credits tied to purchases from one country or company, chiefly from the United States. In 1953 the capitalist states tried to curtail this trade subsidy to the exporting corporations through formal agreement. But like most such agreements, the Americans broke it as soon as it seemed advantageous. Such suppliers' credits in many cases make up the bulk of Third World debt — 63 percent for Brazil, 52 percent for Peru, 90 percent for South Korea, 53 percent for Nigeria, to cite a few examples. It is this form of credit, generally extending for a term of five to eight years, which since the mid-1950s was the "major reason for the need to reschedule the debts of a number of countries, notably Brazil, Chile, Ghana, Indonesia, and Turkey."[15]

Added to the loans of the international institutions and the "suppliers' credits" are the proliferating loans over the past few years made by private banks in the Eurodollar market. In the context discussed in Chapter Three, inevitable future defaults on these debts are likely to have even more serious consequences to the operations of the international capitalist system in that they could set off a collapse in major banks.

The mounting total debts of the Third World only strengthened the power of the Bank and Fund in their efforts to orient national economic policies. Their traditional solution, as evidenced by all the surveillance programs that they have introduced is to increase the level of exploitation of the working population. Supposedly this reduction to even greater destitution will discourage the introduction of machinery, since the cost of labor will be even more marginal. To balance the budget, the first priority is to eliminate subsidies on the necessities of the working class — food, fuel, and public transport. To conserve foreign exchange it is necessary to reduce imports, so they routinely advised curtailing the "propensity to consume" by enlarging export sales and encouraging savings. These measures are reactionary in any situation, but in the context of the preindustrial societies they are absurd. The result uniformly is stagnation and depression. Instead of savings by the small elite such measures generally encourage capital flight. In brief, the IMF, World Bank, and Development Bank's manipulation of the preindustrial economic policies along orthodox lines has led to even greater contradictions and crises than similar efforts in the industrial societies.

The contradictions in this policy are obvious, for at the same time the World Bank and the IMF *want* to achieve "development," as they also desire a crisis-free capitalism. It is simply that the means of the development experts to achieve increased employment, balanced payments and budgets, strong currencies, industrialization, and reduced dependence on imports, are all so regressive that they only compound the problems they are intended to solve. It is inevitable that whenever this form of capitalist "planning" is introduced, in either the industrial or the Third World, conditions are aggravated. The so-called successes, such as the Marshall Plan and the German and Japanese "miracle" economies, were achieved not through direct economic policies but as a result of the impact of war on the world economy, as were the growth rates in the Third World. Otherwise, viewed even from their own perspective, they were disastrous failures in the past, and such effort will continue to be in the future. This is all the more certain in the Third World because any suggestion of a change in the structural base of imperialism, or move toward balanced development, would be in direct conflict with the short-term interests — the only interests which motivate decisions — of the international corporations investing in the Third World only to exploit the cheap workers and to extract raw materials.

### Investment and Trade

The economic conditions of the Third World, intimately linked to the boom and bust cycles of the industrial states, fluctuate even more sharply than the industrial economies. During the Korean war and between 1960 and 1968, which were periods of vast world economic expansion, the annual growth rate of the Third World averaged 5 percent a year. Whenever recession develops in the industrial states, demand for raw materials declines even faster, along with concomitant drops in price and materials gluts. Private profits or government plans, depending on the social organization, suffer accordingly, creating a squeeze on debt repayment and diminishing exports. National income falls but expenses grow. Yet even during the relatively prosperous years of expansion in output, the Third World's share of world trade fell from 21.3 percent in 1960 to 17.6 percent in 1970. For those nations seeking economic development, such problems of raw materials and the cost of required imports from the industrial nations as opposed to the income they receive for their exports — the terms-of-trade — are acute. Even in periods of rising prices for their exports, the terms-of-trade are usually negative as the prices of imports increase even more rapidly.

The major growth factor in Third World exports over the past decade has been in manufactured merchandise. As I discussed in Chapters Two and Four, the pursuit of low-cost labor has led many of the largest corporations of North America and Europe, and now Japan, to set up plants in the Third World to export to the industrial states. The most important developments of this trend have been in Brazil, Mexico, Taiwan, South Korea, Singapore, Malaysia, and the Philippines. The rival efforts among these governments to offer attractive subsidies far exceed anything offered by the European governments during the 1960s. According to the U.N. World Economic Survey, in the period 1959-61 raw materials, other than oil, accounted for 27 percent, and manufacturing 12 percent, of Third World exports to the developed market economies, but by 1967-69 the figures were both equal at 19 percent. Petroleum, on the other hand, had increased from 25 to 32 percent over the same period. In Latin America, manufacturing made up one-half the 1972 capital expenditure, in contrast to one-third in the 1967-71 average. Brazil and Mexico were the major targets. The average increase of exports of the Third World to the industrial capitalist states was 7 percent a year during the 1960s, but with wide variations in content. The export of fuels doubled between 1960 and 1968 but industrial raw materials rose by only 2 percent, "ordinary manufactured goods" rose 2½ times, and machinery, 7 times. Manufactured goods exports as a whole grew 13 percent a year.

There was a substantial shift in the Third World's markets, with Japan becoming increasingly important and Britain declining in equal proportion. During the 1960s the U.S.'s share of total Third World exports to the industrial nations hovered around one-third but declined in raw materials, which dropped "even in absolute terms," comprising 25 percent at the beginning of the decade but only 15 percent in 1966-68. The share of manufactured goods, however, rose by 19 percent a year — or from 8 percent in 1960 of Third World output to over 20 percent by the decade's end. U.S. imports of electronic and telecommunications goods increased by four times between 1965 and 1968. This sector will grow even faster during the 1970s, for all radio and TV manufacturers have deserted America for the Third World.

Japan, on the other hand, imported only 9 percent of the Third World exports in 1960 but by 1968-69 had increased its share to 14 percent. Raw materials made up 40 percent of the total. And while those raw materials are ostensibly from the Third World, the vast bulk are owned by American corporations. It is evident that the highly touted Third World growth rates of an average of 5 percent a year during the 1960s were dependent on the demand and economic activity in the industrial world and the investment of the multinational corporations. This, in turn, as we have seen in earlier chapters, was linked to the war in Vietnam, which generated a high level of demand in the industrial world. Even directly, stimulated largely by U.S. procurement, sales from Taiwan, South Korea, Singapore, and Thailand to South Vietnam increased by three times between 1964 and 1967 to nearly one-quarter billion dollars. But for the Third World the principal increase was the indirect effect of war in creating a generally booming market in the industrial nations.

The growth in aggregate output had nothing to do with real development, for the nature of the internal market distorted the allocation of resources in most areas. Effective demand in most of these countries, because of the extreme inequities in the distribution of the very low per capita income, rests with the small elite, and that inequality has worsened over the past two decades. The imports of these precarious economies are therefore often for luxury goods and have nothing to do with the needs of the population. The much-encouraged "import substitution" programs — building factories to produce goods otherwise imported — are also intended to meet the demands of the elite and these factories tend to be capital-, rather than labor-intensive. The distribution of income obviously is the major factor preventing the growth of a market within the

Third World and all the structural factors in operation can only worsen it.

The industries built for export goods by foreign corporations, besides exploiting the working class, do next to nothing for the financial condition of the countries where they are located, other than providing a marginal contribution to employment. This tends to be very minimal indeed due to the capital intensive character of most of the industries. What with the government subsidies, the artificial low pricing within the multinationals and the repatriation of profits, there is little residue left for the accumulation of capital for more balanced industrialization. The multinational corporations also quickly export more capital than they invest, and increasingly much of the new capital is raised locally, particularly in Latin America. The giant corporations tend to monopolize the local capital market, of course, because they are the safest risks. Otherwise local capital, like all private capital, will seek its most profitable outlet worldwide, either in investment, currency speculation, or interest rates, and hence capital flight is substantial nearly everywhere in the Third World. The Indian corporations Tata, Birla Industries, and others, for example, have 30 projects abroad, such as major chemical works in Argentina, for which they export enormous sums from capital-poor India.

Through their sheer size the multinationals have great discretionary mobility of capital and can rapidly transfer production from one part of the globe to another in search of higher profit. This is particularly true when the motivation is lower wage labor. Private corporations are not interested in employment maximization or development, but in profit. And even if an expanding market in the Third World is in their long-term interest, and in fact essential to it, they will not, except inadvertently, act in such a way as to help to construct it. This is especially true in the Third World where the object is quick and enormous profits in a politically unstable environment. Since cheap labor is the goal of the manufacturing investors, even marginal rises in the labor costs in one area will send them scurrying elsewhere in search of new workers to exploit. This is now true of the electronic corporations, who after several years of operations in Taiwan and South Korea watched wages climb to $1.05 a day and are moving to Malaysia and Indonesia, where wages are 30 cents a day. And as added inducements, Malaysia has offered a free port for industrial imports, allowed full foreign ownership rights, and a ten-year tax holiday.[16] The present circumstances are in a sense a reverse of the earlier imperialist situation when the colonies were to provide the materials and the market to keep the factories in the metropole operating. Now the preindustrial world is providing the capital and manufactured goods for industrial growth and consumption in the industrial sectors of the world.

## Trade and Markets

Most "development" authorities regard trade as the only real basis for future Third World growth. They deem external capital flow as needed but not as crucial. The Pearson report focused on export earnings as the critical means to obtain foreign exchange, for it pointed out that the industrial economies were less eager to provide foreign "aid" by which to bolster reserves. Conscious of this, many Third World states also began at the particularly inopportune time of the 1970-71 recession to orient their economies further toward export. But for the same reasons that capital "aid" declines there are also protectionist pressures in trade which make a large increase in exports rather remote, even though export is certainly the intent of the major investors. Plants established by the state for prestige at great cost will not operate either if there is no market. In fact, in many areas the elaborate industrial infrastructure goes largely unused. For example, 1969-70 was considered an optimum year for production in Pakistan, but the fertilizer industry operated at 79 percent capacity; cotton textile, at 69 percent; petrol, at 45 percent; chemicals, at 18 percent; and nonelectrical machinery, at 14 percent of capacity. And the question remains: where will the demand be found for this vast increase in manufacturing capacity within the existing structure of income distribution and escalating trade wars?

The effective demand for manufactured goods still remains confined to the industrial world, but as demonstrated in earlier chapters, that market is increasingly fragile. The industrial states are already in conflict over trade and have begun scrambling for advantages, even for the limited market of the Third World. "Washington's judicious use of a little muscle is opening up a fast-growing preferential market for U.S. companies in Taiwan . . . [The] U.S. Ambassador . . . has been advising the government . . . that giving the U.S. a better break in trade would help insure continued American political and military support," reported *Business Week* in April 1973. As the Commerce Department sheepishly explained this diplomatic "muscle," "We are treading on dangerous ground . . . . But if we are to meet the competition, we must do some of these things."[17] The Commerce Department hopes that Taiwan's moves will serve as a model for South Korea and other areas increasingly in Japan's trade orbit. And by November 1973, South Korean business had responded to the "Buy American" campaign and ordered nearly $700 million in American goods, about double the year before.

Nevertheless, the economic fate of the Asian Pacific area still rests wholly on the fortunes of Japan, its most important market as well as its chief supplier of industrial goods. The negative terms of trade have indebted the Asian states to the point of $2.2 billion in foreign exchange payments to Japan in 1971, and what with the yen revaluations and the direction of trade, the situation could worsen considerably over the coming years. As the world moves irrevocably toward currency and trade blocs, with restrictions in the giant U.S. market, the area could once more be a center of conflict as it becomes more important to Japan for both trade and investment. Yet Japan has more to lose than gain at the expense of others.

For those countries where the multinational corporations invest in search of cheap labor for the export of parts or finished products, the investment pattern may continue or even accelerate in the first phases of industrial capitalist crisis as the firms of rival nations compete for a shrinking market. It will continue, however, only so long as there is no tariff discrimination against the exports of Third World nations. If that occurs the bulk of the production will shift back to the industrialized countries which will still provide, in the last analysis, the market for production. In other words, at a certain point the vast expansion of Third World manufacturing capacity will fall idle.

The problems will obviously be acute for the compradore capitalist states whose answer to popular unrest is, and will remain, unabashed repression. Nevertheless, such consequences will be politically serious in countries where development has advanced the farthest and expectations, thereby, have become the greatest. For the more progressive mixed economies in the Third World are no less dependent on the world capitalist market for their development than the purely compradore states.

### Raw Materials

The question of the importance of raw materials in the Third World to the industrialized nations has been exhaustively discussed elsewhere, ranging from the history of wars fought for access to supplies to lesser crises. Japan and Western Europe, less well endowed in these essentials of industrial power than the U.S. or the U.S.S.R., have always responded to any *real* threat of a loss of critical needs. For most of the Third World nations possession of raw materials has been, at once, a benefit and a bane, and for those lacking the essential supplies, access to them is a critical part of their dependence. Since these crucial factors are now widely understood, it suffices here only to point out some dimensions of the raw materials question that are often overlooked.

While there has been a substantial shift in investment and trade from raw materials (oil excepted) to manufactured products over the past decade, by 1970 almost one-half the Third World countries received more than 50 percent of their export income from one primary product and three-fourths received 60 percent from only three or less commodities. Their largest single market for raw materials is Japan, followed at a substantial distance by the U.S. The U.S. is still the largest importer of food from the Third World, absorbing over one-third of the $9 billion market of chiefly tropical, American corporation-owned, products. Not only does the U.S. economy as a whole consume

40 percent of the world's nonrenewable resources, a large part of which is produced domestically, but those consumed by others are largely purchased from American corporations.

Demand, exploration, and growth in output of these primary products depend on economic conditions in the industrial capitalist states, and demand and prices are usually the first casualty in any downward shift in the economic forecasts or activity in the industrial world, just as they are the beneficiary of expanding industrial economies. In 1973, when demand was high, there was widespread concern over the shortage of certain raw materials, in particular oil, which innumerable experts have projected onto the next 10 to 20 years, predicting that the U.S. will be "forced" to import 51 percent of its oil needs by 1985. The impact on the balance-of-payments, the new shift in world power relations, struggles for the control of supplies by the various capitalist states, are not merely conjectured but are in fact under way, especially since the Mideast war in October 1973. For in the short run, the mere general anticipation of a future shortage of so important a material as petroleum sets in motion massive, and successful, rival efforts at exploration and political jockeying to secure supplies through separate arrangements with oil-producing states.

It is true that if the industrial economies were to operate at full capacity for the next 10 to 20 years there could be acute shortages of many of the essential materials. But how likely is that fundamental precondition? In the context of the previous discussions in this book it would be rash indeed to isolate the question of today's high demand for raw materials from the rest of the developments in the world political economy. It is, in fact, essential to link all discussions of the supply of raw materials to the global political-economic system. In a capitalist society, therefore, there is no such thing as an absolute shortage or an absolute surplus — there is less a raw materials problem than there is a capitalist problem. Raw materials demand follows the business cycle and fluctuates even more wildly. Yet the tendency to project into the future on the basis of immediate conditions still prevails.

An interesting illustration of this propensity is Sidney

Dell's excellent study, *Trade Blocs and Common Markets,* written in 1962. Referring to the report of the President's Commission on Raw Materials prepared in 1952, Dell writes, "The Paley Commission's idea of a long-term and unprecedented raw material shortage seems laughable in the economic climate today. With almost all agricultural and mineral products in surplus supply, it appears scarcely credible that such views could have been advanced on such high authority only ten years ago."[18]  Superficially, one might say the same of Dell in 1973, when a shortage of supplies was generally feared.  To be more than superficial, however, one must calculate other factors in the world economy.  The shortage hysteria, particularly in oil, of the early 1950s was induced by the war in Korea, and followed a period of surplus.  It, in turn, attracted a large amount of capital for exploration and development, further increased by the Suez crisis, leading to an oversupply which the sharp downturn in economic activity in the U.S. in 1958 aggravated.  With the war in Vietnam, of course, the situation was once more reversed. The war was immensely profitable for the oil industry, for not only did it literally fuel the world economic boom that was an outcome of the war, but direct sales to the U.S. military in Vietnam, chiefly from the Middle East, rose to $500 million in 1968 in contrast to total military purchases of $265 million annual average between 1960 and 1965.  These figures apply to overseas expenditures only.  But by September 1967 there were again loud outcries over ". . . a possible critical oversupply of domestic crude."[19]  Then, by April 1969 demand was again "devouring" supply and a shortage was feared.[20]  With the recession of 1970, the *Oil and Gas Journal* announced that "Demand for Petroleum to Slow with Economy."[21]  In 1972-73 the world economy was operating at near peak capacity and there were political pressures on the oil companies from the Arab states. The oil industry "majors" also had a long-standing desire to raise the U.S. import quotas on the more profitable foreign oil and increase prices generally.  There ensued a near-hysterical campaign on the dangers of a world oil shortage.

A Federal Trade Commission 1973 report of an investigation of the industry laid the shortages to a collusion of the major companies to destroy the independents. The government had lifted all anti-trust restrictions on the oil companies in 1971 supposedly so that they could better respond to OPEC. The conclusion of the two-year FTC study was that the oil companies "have attempted to increase profits by restricting output [and] . . . have used the shortage as an occasion to debilitate, if not eradicate, the independent marketing sector."[22] Despite such reports, the ensuing hysteria of an energy shortage focused everywhere but on the companies themselves. After the State Department modified its position on Middle-East policies and the import barriers were lowered, the head of the Petroleum Industry Research Foundation declared in September 1973 that there was indeed no world shortage of crude but only the U.S. was suffering. In fact, he noted, the Arabs were not restricting sales to the U.S. and that the Mideast, including Iran, provided only 7.4 percent of U.S. supplies. What, then, was the problem? The remaining issue was insufficient refining capacity caused by restrictions of the anti-pollution laws — and the subsequent target of the oil industry's campaign.[23] The war in the Middle East in October 1973 again changed this perspective as the Arab states began to boycott shipments to the U.S., and the Europeans invoked restrictions on the export of refined oil, leading to restrictions on the more important Canadian oil to the U.S. This stimulated moves to expand production in U.S. reserves and talk of rationing, dealt a blow to the conservationists and cleared opposition to an Alaska pipeline, and raised the price of oil — all oil industry goals over the preceding months. The boycott also heightened political tensions between the U.S. and Western Europe. The oil companies, meanwhile, were reaping record profits. For the Arab states it was fortunate that the world economy was still operating at near peak capacity, as their political leverage depended on that fact. Nevertheless, between writing and publishing these words the world's evaluation of the oil shortage may once again be transformed.

In the case of the other raw materials, recent experience again underlines the fact that the adequacy of supplies is conditioned on trends in world economic activity. There is no

shortage of illustrations of this rule.  In November 1971 the
*Wall Street Journal* reported on the "Commodities Collapse."
With the recession in the industrial world, inventories were
reduced on a global basis, bringing depression to many
commodity-dependent countries.  Prices had plunged over the
year:  nickel by eight times, rubber to its lowest point in eight
years, cocoa by 50 percent, with similar trends in tin, lead, platinum, copper, and all the minerals essential for steel, which was
also in a serious slump.  As for the future, one London banker
was quoted as forecasting that "There's nothing in sight to help
the commodity market, and there are a lot of things that could
depress it even further."[24]  Exactly one year later the *New
York Times* reported that the present and projected shortage of
these same minerals ". . . helps explain the much tougher bar-
gaining position recently taken by poor-country governments. . . ."[25]  Yet scarcely fearing shortages, in March 1973
the U.S. government decided to dump precipitously nearly
$5 billion of its $6.5 billion raw material stockpile in order to
deflate prices.

Availability in the U.S., prodded by the level of economic
activity, reflects other factors as well, such as new discoveries,
technological developments, substitutions, synthetics, the condition of processing plants, anti-pollution measures, and price
differentials that can all affect the condition of supply of natural
resources.  New discoveries of lead and copper in the U.S. expanded earlier reserves estimates of the early 1950s up to
fivefold.  Recently, exploration on the ocean floor has turned
up a vast array of "nodules," rich in the scarce minerals of
manganese, cobalt, nickel, as well as copper.  U.S. corporations
are now investing millions in exploration and extraction but
most of the efforts are cloaked in secrecy since the legal ramifications as to who owns the ocean floor are unresolved.  Technology of offshore drilling expanded oil supplies greatly, and
the technology of recycling has also increased available resources.  Copper companies, responding to antipollution regulations, are threatening to cut back their U.S. production
sharply, increasing "dependence" on imports.  Closing seven
antiquated zinc smelters increased import needs for that

metal. And devaluation, on the other hand, increased costs of imports, and substitutions are beginning to reduce the market. Prices of many raw materials due to "ample supplies" have hardly risen on a long-term basis, although they have fluctuated widely on the short-term. Lead prices in 1973 were the same as in 1948, aluminum was the same as in 1960, and iron prices rose less than 10 percent in 12 years. Price controls in 1973 on industrial supplies in the U.S. led producers to export them for the higher prices abroad, creating shortages in America — and consequent imports of these same materials. Higher prices, in turn, are expected to stimulate substitution, recycling, and exploration. But, of course, even ample U.S. supplies of a raw material in no way insure a country against economic, political, or military intervention if it threatens American property. For even if 100 percent of production is destined for a third country, or if no raw materials are involved, the U.S. will intervene in some form, depending on the economic environment and the power of the corporation and country concerned, not only to maintain access to vital materials, but equally to protect a banana plantation of United Fruit, a telecommunications network of ITT, a copper mine of Kennecott Corporation, or any other corporate interest.

For the corporation investing in the Third World for raw materials the primary motive, regardless of availability, will be to search for the cheapest source possible, not for the buyer but for higher profit margins for the extracting corporation. And this pursuit of lower labor costs is more fundamental than scarcity or the availability of certain minerals. The long-standing aim of the major oil companies to import cheaper Mideast supplies is not to provide the consumer with lower-priced fuel but to reap greater profits with higher priced fuels. While the oil companies were restricting supply to create shortages over the past two years and applying political pressures to import cheaper Mideast oil, the subsequent political developments in the Mideast may raise royalties to the point where the cost differential with domestic supplies disappears. Under these circumstances the rising retail price, blamed on the oil sheiks, more than compensates by roughly ten to one for the royalty increase. This rise only further fuels inflation and increases costs across the economy at an important juncture in the world economy.[26]

It cannot be said that the Third World is subsidizing the industrial economies *per se.* They, or rather their workers, are subsidizing foreign corporations that, through the higher degree of exploitation of labor, are reaping higher profits. Even if raw materials are nationalized it is the owning corporation that is adversely affected, not the buyers. There is no reason to believe the cost to the buyer will be higher. The corporations sell their materials for what the market will bear, at prices generally set on an exchange in London. The differential between cost and price is not a subsidy to the buyer but is the differential of corporate profit. The notable exception, of course, is when manufacturing corporations seek their own supply of cheap raw materials, such as the symbiotic links between iron mining and steel producers. The price of Bethlehem Steel's Brazilian iron will reflect only intracorporate price manipulations for tax advantage, but its real costs will be considerably less than buying iron from another corporation, American or not. Copper from Chile was imported at low cost and sold at high cost, and the same was true of imported oil from the Middle East. Otherwise, sales to other corporations of any nationality will reflect what the market will bear.

Despite the importance of trends in the world economy on supplies and prices, obviously there still remains an absolute need of certain countries for a number of indispensable raw materials even at a very low level of economic activity. Japan must import 99 percent of its oil, and 100 percent of its uranium, nickel, and alumina, 96 percent of its tin, 88 percent of its iron, and 76 percent of its copper. The EEC countries import 96 percent of their oil as well as other vital supplies, and the U.S., comparatively well endowed, must import more than one-half of a growing list of industrial minerals — by 1970, 6 of the 13 primary minerals — and the bulk of these supplies comes from the Third World.[27] And although, by and large, this relationship does not mean that the industrial economies are in any way threatened by the fact that they must import,

since, for the foreseeable future, it is much more critical that
the nations of the Third World export, the 1973 experience
with an oil boycott reveals that at least the oil-producing states,
during a period of high level of world economic activity, have
considerable political power in the critical realm of energy for
Europe and Japan. But with their swollen monetary reserves
to purchase essential imports and their small population, their
position is unique in the Third World. A real struggle evolved
between the industrial nations during this time, and whatever
solidarity may have existed among them on the question of
energy before the boycott crumbled as each industrial nation
determined to seek its own solution. One may imagine that
it could even lead to some industrial states encouraging nationalization and promising a guaranteed market. With economic
conflict in every aspect of their relations, the oil crisis only
accentuated the tension. At present there is a frenetic search
for new supplies and development of alternatives. But since
the capitalist states are not planned economies this will go on
only as long as there is a shortage. With the decline in economic activity, and ironically the manipulated shortage may
have been the decisive push toward recession, an oil surplus
would reduce, if not eliminate altogether, such efforts. Most
of the anxious Presidential commission studies and other dire
predictions dissolve during economic slowdowns. The struggle
for raw materials may be transitional, but it is no less intense
thereby — reactions, in fact, may be so strong as to lead to
war.

Nevertheless, the rest of the Third World lacks such power
as the oil producers and is extremely vulnerable at all times,
for the reasons discussed earlier in this chapter, to the developments in the industrial nations. They must export their resources for the highest price available, even if controlled by a
revolutionary government instead of a private foreign corporation. The Third World nations themselves, while they account
for a good part of the trade in raw materials, depend on foreign corporations for their own supplies of essential materials,
and in periods of rising prices are the first to feel the squeeze.

The fluctuation in demand for minerals and agricultural

products has, of course, varying impact on the Third World, depending on the social organization of the country involved. Clearly an oil glut for Saudi Arabia or Kuwait merely means a fluctuation in their financial reserves of perhaps a few billion dollars. There is certainly a point of satiety of luxuries for the ruling clique, long since attained. For the population, a surplus or shortage is quite irrelevant.

A copper surplus and the fall in prices, on the other hand, has a much wider impact on the state-controlled economies of Zambia, Peru, and, before the military coup d'etat, Chile. In 1971 the fall in copper prices reduced the revenue of the government of Zambia 15 percent and its foreign reserves fell by one-third in 12 months. In Chile copper amounted to 88 percent of its export earnings. While the impact on the whole society can be readily seen in the more progressive states of the Third World, there is no reason whatever to believe that they will be less dependent on the fluctuations in the markets of the industrial capitalist states.

Rational exploitation of world reserves would depend on a different kind of economic system allocating their development according to need. As it is, it depends on the corporations' estimate of profitability. More pointedly, the problem is less one of actual scarcity, for there appears to be much agreement that there are plenty of materials, but rather who is to exploit them? Those economists able to isolate economic growth figures from the context of the general political economy are also able to project massive shortages into the future. In many instances they are sincere, if narrow, in their analysis; in other cases they are spokesmen for industries seeking special subsidies or dispensations from import quotas, anti-pollution laws, or anti-trust regulations.

Nothing expresses so well the total irrationality of capitalist production and distribution than the violent swings from surplus to scarcity in food. In December 1971 the U.S. was trying to persuade the EEC to curtail grain output, and there was a "surplus" of rice, even in India, and restricted output and depression in Asia, while millions were hungry, because there was no "effective" demand. But in one year unfavorable weather drove prices beyond the reach of even "effective" demand and a world food shortage was proclaimed. There were bread riots in Naples and rice riots in the Philippines and India in August 1973.[28] New incentives for production were introduced, famine relief efforts considered on a world scale, and the cycle began once more.

Capitalists are no more able to reflect and act on the fact that raw materials fluctuate from glut to scarcity every few years, to which they respond with policies of expansive development and exploration to subsidized curtailment of supplies, any more than they reflect on their experiences with other aspects of capitalist "planning" dealing with fiscal and monetary policies. Their myopia is simply one more element of the irrational and crisis-inducing features inherent in the system itself.

### Conclusion

For the Third World governments that aim at national economic development within the world capitalist system there is only a treadmill of compounded debt, increasing dependence, and capital drain. The old status quo has been fractured by structural changes of the past two decades through urbanization that radically uprooted the social foundation of centuries in agrarian societies and created massive unemployment without the potential of integrating this immense rootless population into an industrial proletariat. The needs nearly everywhere are awesome, and the restraints to even moderate reform are monumental.

All development must be under the auspices of the state, and can only succeed after breaking out of the web of entangling debts and market dependence as well as locating new suppliers of essential imports. But as the entire postwar experience shows, this is an extraordinarily difficult, if not impossible, goal within the context of the international capitalist system. When there is resistance or even hints of a will to break out of the imperialist bonds, or merely acts of despair, the reaction is swift. When the international solidarity of the control of credits, essential imports, and markets does not succeed in forcing conformity, the reaction is violence, usually backed by the world's most powerful single nation.

Since the Second World War, much of the Third World has been the battlefield and the recipient of the most systematic intense violence and class repression, the laboratory of vicious weapons systems, police techniques, and extreme exploitation. In addition to barbarous wars in Korea and Indochina, millions have been murdered in counterrevolution — or more accurately, "anticipatory" counterrevolution — on the mere suspicion of threatening property relations, or for simply being members of the wrong class. Immense numbers in many nations are vulnerable by their very permanent superfluousness to the process of production, both on the land and in the urban areas to which they have fled. They face a dangerous and terrible future if the forces of the status quo endure. Since World War II there have been at least six other wars associated with the interests of one or another industry in Indonesia, Algeria, Malaysia, Nigeria, the Philippines, and the Congo. At least nine major coups d'etat against reformist governments, followed by bloody repression and rapid concessions to threatened international capitalist interests, have defined the societies of Indonesia, Guatemala, Iran, Brazil, Argentina, Chile, Greece, and the Dominican Republic. The list of other violent repressions is as long as the fears of the ruling cliques and the interests behind them in their efforts to create the "infrastructure" of security. Millions today experience this condition of terror as well as exploitation. And shaping that reality, as well, are the economic policies of the ruling compradores under the guidance of the economic experts in "development" who, over the past two decades, have gravely aggravated rather than alleviated the endemic problems of these preindustrial countries. This is the irreducible context for any understanding of the economic condition of the Third World today.

### CHAPTER SIX

# THE SOVIET BLOC, CHINA, AND THE
# CAPITALIST CRISIS

> . . . if in order to serve one's narrow national interests, one
> is to help the most reactionary forces stave off dangerous blows,
> one is indeed throwing a life-buoy to a drowning pirate; this is
> a harmful compromise advantageous to the enemy, and disad-
> vantageous to the revolution. *Nhan Dan,* August 17, 1972.

Faced with conflict in trade, a near saturation in
effective demand both in the industrial states and
the Third World, and a burgeoning productive
capacity, many of the world's capitalists believed
by the 1970s that they literally had no option but to look
covetously at the vast potential market in the orderly economies of the Soviet bloc and China. In 1972 these appeared
the only areas of the world where there remained a possibility
of expansive and complementary economic relationships.

## *The Soviet "Life-buoy"*
One of the most critical explanations for the 1972 shift in
American business confidence and the expansionary direction
of the economy was the new turn in trade relations with the Soviet bloc and China. Pressures from the chief foreign trade-oriented
industrial corporations and major American banks to evolve a
new relationship had been mounting for some years. Yet as
late as May 1970 the U.S. government vetoed Ford's participation in the huge Kama River truck plant. It took the acute
economic crisis of 1971 to jar the Nixon Administration loose
from its archaic ideological moorings and set it firmly on its

new paths. For the Nixon Administration there also appeared the political benefit of using the lure of trade and better relations to isolate the Vietnamese from their chief suppliers and thereby forestall the inevitable American defeat in that war-ravaged country.

At the end of World War II the Soviet Union was prepared to cooperate with the United States on matters of trade, and, for a time, U.S. policy-makers were interested in an attempt to integrate the Russians into their plan for the world economy. There had even been some beginnings during the 1930s. But certain critical factors made Russia's integration impossible in the postwar years. Due to the devastation of the war in Europe, the U.S. was cut off from its former markets because of an acute foreign exchange shortage on the part of its potential capitalist trade partners. Only the American government could, in the short run, provide the dollars for the rest of the world to buy its goods. The scarcity of dollars was also leading to new, state-managed trade between the western and eastern sectors of Europe, which, from the U.S. point of view, threatened to become permanent and thereby exclude U.S. goods from this important area of foreign commerce. Moreover, the Americans still hoped for a semi-colonial role for East Europe. What was clearly mandatory for the American system by 1947 was a bloc of capitalist states as a recipient of dollar grants to finance immediately American trade while simultaneously reconstructing a prosperous market for future business. It was, in an important degree, an emergency, but obtaining the funds required the circuitous route of Congress which, as a bastion of unreflective ideology, not only would not make grants to the U.S.S.R. but needed a high-pitched, anti-communist rationale to vote the grants for capitalist Europe. Anti-Soviet ideology is certainly agreeable to America's more sophisticated leaders, but only so long as it serves their interests. The so-called "Cold War" set the framework of those interests for more than two decades and two wars. Meanwhile, the events over those years were fundamentally changing the American capitalists' relations with the rest of the world and, in particular, the other capitalist states. The dollar shortage had become a glut, Western Europeans were highly competitive, fully recovered, and the capitalist world in general was facing seemingly insoluble problems of inflation, overproduction, and a keen competition for markets and lower costs that was evolving into another major crisis for world capitalism as a system. On the sidelines of this developing struggle were the two vast potential markets of the Soviet bloc and China, artificially excluded because of the now counterproductive ideological quarantine. It was inevitable that as the crisis intensified between the capitalist powers there would be an "opening to the East." The Western Europeans had already advanced far along this path. Although the Russians enjoyed Most-Favored-Nation (MFN) treatment with the U.S. from 1935-51, after 1951 U.S.-Soviet trade virtually came to a halt. However, between 1955 and 1970 Soviet trade with Western Europe grew from 21 to 35 percent of total Soviet trade.[1] This shift in relations with the U.S. was made all the more certain by the juncture of interests on the part of the Russian and Chinese managers, prodded by the economic difficulties within their own system, and who, after all, had always been the defensive parties. Once their interest in expanded economic ties was revealed, action followed swiftly. It is difficult to overestimate the importance of this new turn.

### The American Interests

From the American viewpoint, one can easily calculate the enormous benefits for individual industries and the general economy accruing from the new relations with the Soviet Union and, to a lesser extent, with China. It is no wonder that one industry after another celebrated the new relations as Nixon's greatest achievement of his first four years and, most significantly, such acclaim comes from the most powerful U.S. industries and banking interests.

Starting in July 1972 with "history's biggest" single grain trade agreement, a $750 million transaction that may exceed $1 billion over three years, U.S. industries have moved with alacrity to secure their own contracts. The grain deal had wide ramifications, many of which were unforeseen and are still emerging over two years later. When the agreement was made there was a surplus of wheat in the U.S. and falling prices. Britain, one of the American farmer's major markets, was about to enter the EEC — a trade-bloc which had already reduced its U.S. agricultural imports by 40 percent over four years. Agricultural interests have always been an important factor in American foreign policy and, particularly in an election year, such an accord, unprecedented in volume, was welcome indeed to the Administration. Forty percent of U.S. total wheat sales in fiscal 1973 were to the Soviet Union, as well as 25 percent of its feed grains. Such a massive sale sparked "a boom" in other related and sluggish sectors of the economy, such as railroads, shipping, ports activity, new orders for railroad cars, river traffic, and the like: ". . . the massive export of grain is giving the U.S. economy a tremendous boost," was the opinion of *U.S. News and World Report.*[2]   Yet aside from the alleged political graft involved for Continental Grain, there were inherent contradictions in the sale in a situation which within a year evolved into the skyrocketing prices that, coupled with unfavorable global weather conditions, produced a world shortage in grain, scarcities in meat, and famine in many areas.

### Oil and Gas

News of the most spectacular U.S.-Soviet trade deal began to emerge in November 1972 when it became known that multi-billion dollar barter contracts were being negotiated to develop the oil and gas fields of Siberia. One involved the development of the Yakutsk region in eastern Siberia to supply Japan and the West coast of the U.S. And in June 1973 the Soviets signed an agreement with a consortium of Occidental Petroleum and El Paso Natural Gas providing for a preliminary 25-year contract for $10 billion. The Japanese may join the project in the future. The deal requires an initial Western loan of $4 billion to construct a pipeline and a tanker fleet.

Even larger, however, is an agreement involving western

Siberia which barters natural gas in return for $12.5 billion in goods and services over a 25-year period. Negotiating this contract was a Texan consortium of Texas Eastern Transmission, Tenneco, and Brown & Root. This massive accord was signed with the U.S.S.R. on June 29, 1973, with the direct encouragement of President Nixon. Involved in the financing of the transaction is a consortium of banks led by Citibank and Bank of America. *The Oil and Gas Journal* reported that the State Department regards ". . . it as desirable diversification of foreign energy sources and a hedge against loss of Middle East or African imports."[3]  The projects were purported to contribute millions of man-hours of employment in the U.S. since the gas will be sold for credits for Soviet purchases in America.

The U.S. has both the money to invest and the market for natural resources, especially oil and gas, at this particular moment in its history. The money invested and loaned would be used to buy goods in America, spreading the benefits across the entire economy, increasing employment, and improving the balance-of-payments. The Soviets were to repay the development loans with natural resources and at the same time expand their own internal consumer market. The recent Kremlin policy decision to sell the natural resources of Siberia opened prospects of trade and repayment on a massive scale which did not exist when Soviet exports were perceived as only crabmeat, caviar, vodka, and the like. At the June 1972 summit meeting in Moskow, Brezhnev described the Siberian riches — probably the world's largest petroleum deposits — to Nixon and showed him a map of "This wealth that we are prepared to share with you."[4] An article in *Pravda* underlined Russia's interest in these prospects: "Mutually advantageous cooperation between Soviet organizations and American firms in developing . . . natural resources . . . could, in our opinion, be one of the most promising paths. . . [and] would create a lasting and long-term basis for expanding Soviet-American trade and economic . . . ties . . . ."[5]

The U.S.S.R. has a good proportion of the world's supply of other essential materials as well:  40 percent of the world's iron ore, 60 percent of the world's coal — and it produces 16 percent of the world's copper, 12 percent of its zinc, 15 percent of its lead, 20 percent of its nickel, as well as chromium, platinum, and manganese, and contains one-third of the earth's forests. "Indeed," according to the *Bankers Magazine,* "there is hardly a mineral resource known to man that the Soviet Union does not have in enormous quantities."[6]

Financing the exploitation of these minerals, particularly gas and oil, will be a gigantic project, but it is one which the Americans feel that only they can undertake. "Nothing so large has been tried before in world trade," said then Secretary of Commerce Peterson in the fall of 1972.[7] Just a couple of deals such as the oil and gas projects, he added, would wipe out the Export-Import Bank's capacity of only $4 billion. In March 1973 the ExIm Bank extended the first credit of $100 million to the U.S.S.R. It was matched by private U.S. banks for 90 percent financing for purchases in the U.S. to total $225 million. Most of the huge sums, of course, will come from private investors. Washington officials and bankers expect bond issues "of a magnitude rarely before underwritten."[8] Goldman, Sachs opened a Washington office in the last months of 1972 for the purpose of dealing in the Soviet bonds. The chairman of the New York Stock Exchange went to Moscow in November 1972 to discuss the bond issues with Russian bankers and trade officials.

### The Banks

In quest of the financing of the multiple and ever-expanding agreements between the Soviet Union and the U.S. corporations are the largest American banks. At a time when banks feel forced by competition to grant ever more risky loans around the world at marginal rates, the promise of Eastern Europe, with its ultimate stability and security, was a welcome blessing. "This provides a new business frontier for most U.S. banks," reflected the *Bankers Magazine* with satisfaction in mid-1972.[9] David Rockefeller toured Eastern Europe in January 1973 and shortly thereafter Chase Manhattan won permission to set up a representative office. Thereafter, a rush of "eight to ten" western bankers a day, according to the president of Manufacturers Hanover Trust, began to visit the Soviet central bank in the hope of financing East-West trade.[10]  And inevitable rate-cutting started as Chase was rumored to have offered concessions in lending rates to get the largest possible portion of the business, and continued until interest margins barely allowed any profit.

Many other industries have secured contracts, some at difficult periods in their corporate lives.  International Harvester was pulled out of the red by a Soviet order; General Electric has signed an agreement with the U.S.S.R. for a joint research and development project in nuclear reactors and gas turbines.  General Motors is negotiating for another truck plant in Siberia, one supposed to be far larger than the Kama River $2 billion project.  Control Data signed a ten-year agreement of up to $500 million for joint computer development.  For every agreement already signed there are scores of corporations, including IBM, Boeing, General Dynamics, RCA, ITT, Reynolds Metal, Kaiser, Hewlett Packard, Litton Industries, Alliance Tool and Die, Caterpillar Tractor, and Gulf and Western Industries, bidding for the multiple projects authorized or contemplated in the U.S.S.R.  As the Assistant Secretary of State commented, "It seems that nearly every time we open the *Wall Street Journal* or turn to the financial section of the *Times,* we find a new project with the U.S.S.R. discussed or announced."[11]

One measure of the importance of this new trend was seen in July 1973, after Brezhnev's visit to the U.S., when David Kendall of PepsiCo called a meeting to establish a U.S.-U.S.S.R. Chamber of Commerce and only the presidents or board chairmen of 24 of the largest American industrial and financial corporations were invited to attend.  Companies such as GE, GM, IBM, DuPont, Xerox, Bank of America, Armco Steel, Singer, Continental Grain, Textron, Pan Am, Occidental, and the like were represented.

### Investment and Production in the Eastern Bloc

Within each nation in the Soviet bloc every country has

its own distinctive regulations for foreign investment and production. Rumania permits 49 percent foreign ownership, but Russia permits none whatsoever, while Poland is receptive only if it is the sole means to attract capital. But the U.S. corporations are less concerned about such formalities. They are either following the path of the European and Japanese companies before them or are working out in detail new modes of profit-taking and control of production that are at once highly acceptable to themselves and which do not offend the sensibilities of Leninist precepts. In any case, such practices as joint ventures, leasing, royalties and the like are already familiar, particularly in the Third World. In Eastern Europe there is at least stability, and profit by any name can smell as sweet. On the level of production, the western corporations are interested in both the export and the domestic market. For the export of goods produced in East Europe it is the stability (meaning no strikes) and low labor costs that is attractive to the industries from the strike-torn West. Some MNCs are studying the possibilities of producing in East Europe "high labor content parts and components" for assembly elsewhere.[12]  Such arrangements were already common among West European industries by the beginning of 1972. Pechiney produces aluminum in Hungary; Dutch clothing manufacturers produce in Poland, Hungary, and Rumania; the Swedes and Danes construct furniture in Poland; Italian bathroom equipment is made in Hungary. From the point of view of the Western capitalist, Eastern Europe performs the same function as the Third World or Spain. For the domestic market the interest in production is generally a share in sales, licensing, royalties, and the like.

### The U. S. Government and Economic Ties

In a keynote speech to the World Trade Institute in New York in November 1972, Willis Armstrong, Assistant Secretary of State for Economic and Business Affairs, spoke on "A New Era for East-West Trade." Dealing with the critical concern of his audience over the long-term political stability of the "New Era" and the role of the U.S. government, he said,

> What you as businessmen are seeking . . . is the promise of future stability in Soviet-U.S. relations. You need to make long-term business plans and commitments which are risky enough without having to take account of an inherently immeasurable political factor. This is the same argument we heard from the Soviet trade officials during the negotiations. They, too, insist on a stable future if they are to hinge their industrial buildup on American technology and their export production plans on the U.S. market.

Referring to the new economic agreements between the two countries, Armstrong noted that they

> . . . demarcate a new spirit of U.S. Government encouragement for East-West trade, one which has found wide public support and one which is based on improved mutual understanding between the two governments. . . . These programs are leading us into a stage of practical forms of intimate cooperation with the Soviet Union for years ahead. . . . We [the U.S. government] will give a hand to plans for industrial cooperation that will join us in long-term raw material extractive projects. The mutual interest in insulating these investments against ephemeral political bumps and jolts is self-evident . . . . We are shifting our budget priorities and the Department of Commerce is undertaking its new programs because we think this is the time for American business to make its move in eastern Europe. . . . American assets . . . include . . . a scale of operation that is large enough to be suited to the massive investment approach of the planned economies. . . .

He concluded that "The government's attitude, heretofore ambiguous, is now one of encouragement. We are expanding our services to give you every possible support in promoting this market."[13]  And according to Kenneth Rush, Deputy Secretary of State, "We encourage [American business] to sell, invest, and buy in these countries . . . and in confidence that doing business in eastern Europe is fully consonant with the U.S. national interest."[14]

The U.S. government is working hard to achieve the environment of long-term economic relations and it has repeatedly tested the U.S.S.R. on a political level and found them cooperative. Widely discussed in official and business circles was the meeting between Secretary of Commerce Peterson and the Soviet Trade Minister Nikolai Patolichev the evening Nixon announced the mining of Haiphong harbor and the intensified bombing of the DRV. After watching the President on TV, as Peterson told the editor of *Nation's Business* who accompanied him to Moscow,

> . . . the Russians did not grab their hats and stalk out — as some Americans might have expected. . . . Instead they quietly began speaking again about . . . joint U.S.-Soviet business ventures, loans, interest rates, old debts, shipping arrangements, patents, licensing, copyrights, trademarks, arbitration of disputes, and facilities for U.S. companies setting up shop in the Soviet Union. From that moment, it was obvious that the United States and the Soviet Union would eventually make a deal for major trade expansion. To make certain everyone caught on to this, Patolichev and President Nixon met later in the White House for 45 minutes. They talked about commerce and how their two countries needed each other's business, and they even joked for the cameramen to show they weren't mad at anybody.[15]

The Moscow summit went on as scheduled and major trade agreements followed quickly. This attitude of self-interest was carefully noted by the U.S. government. The Russians may later regret the future dangers to their own security in this form of appeasement, but for the moment they have correctly assessed that the top U.S. business and political leaders are also anxious to make long-term and mutually profitable deals with them.

In June 1973 the House Foreign Affairs Committee released a report with their assessment of the new relations with the U.S.S.R. They also found that the Russians' "moderation" was attested to by their response to mining the harbors and the massive bombing of the DRV, the elimination of the tax on Jewish emigrants, and the Soviet's response to the Watergate revelations. Further reinforcing this favorable view were the agreements on Lend Lease, the Polish decision to make a settlement on prewar government bonds, and Hungarian compensation for property nationalized in the 1940s.

The new detente was, according to the vice-president of Chase Manhattan bank, "born out of necessity." "Let's be quite honest," he amplified. "We do have a balance-of-payments problem and we have to look for new markets."[16]  And as Deputy Secretary of State Kenneth Rush noted in April 1973, "At a time when we have a trade deficit with most areas of the world, our balance of trade surplus with eastern Europe is particularly welcome."[17]

While the greatest proportion of trade and investment remains in the traditional capitalist markets, the U.S. corporations and government find them increasingly competitive and full of conflict, torn by inflation and business cycles of growing severity.  In the Third World, as discussed in Chapter Five, the market is distinctly limited and becoming more so with the aggravation of all its endemic problems over the past decades. By contrast, the Soviet bloc in the eyes of American capitalists is a market of vast potential growth, trade with which will yield a surplus in payments, an enormous reservoir of unexploited natural resources, and a stable, strike-free production environment

In shaping overall policy neither the corporations nor the government contemplate the fact that trade with the Communist countries may be a small proportion of overall trade any more than they dwell on the fact that foreign trade is only 5 percent of the U.S. GNP —and therefore should supposedly be unimportant in American foreign policy.  Those interested in new markets can hardly reflect on the past, when the U.S.S.R. and China were virtually excluded from all trade with the U.S. More germane to the current interests of American consumer industry is the low per capita consumption of goods in the U.S.S.R. contrasted to the nearly saturated market and the rising tariffs and other barriers in those areas with which the U.S. presently has the greatest percentage of its foreign trade. The critical factor leading to a change in American political policy *vis-à-vis* the U.S.S.R. is which industries are interested and why.  By their own account, the most powerful American industries believe that new relations with the Soviet bloc are important for markets, sources of raw materials, safe loans, and the production of goods.  Such economic intercourse is also important to the Soviet rulers, and this fact is no less interesting to us here.  That the Western capitalists will all fail in this goal, as they have in their other efforts, is another question entirely and reflects neither their intentions nor the overall patterns in their trade, but the contradictions in capitalism itself. But for Western capitalism in the 1970s there are no real options for an expanding market — save the artificial government stimulus of an expanded war economy, the contradictions of which I have discussed in the preceding chapters. But despite the best laid plans of the most powerful members of the ruling class and the full cooperation of the Nixon Administration, Congress was able to block or stall the promised MFN provision and the ExIm Bank credits. The long nurtured ideological biases are not so easily erased among those who lack direct economic interests. Those with power eventually will make their will felt, but it involves a struggle and the mere process of stalling may dampen Soviet enthusiasm and encourage them to look elsewhere for their economic desires.

### Soviet Interests

The benefits to the U.S.S.R. from the new relations with the U.S. are equally apparent even if more complex to describe. First, it must be reiterated that the Soviet Union was always the defensive party in the so-called Cold War with the West. A devastated nation at the end of the Second World War, Russia was eager to participate in any American-sponsored reconstruction program, short of one that required dismantling its social system. However, the times were inopportune and the needs of American capitalism were better served by portraying Russia, despite all its efforts to prove otherwise, as the center of revolutionary communism and subversion — in fact, the convenient scapegoat on which to heap all the crises of the postwar world.

The process of accumulating capital to transform a vast underdeveloped agrarian society into the world's second industrial power in 50 years is a grim one under the best of conditions. But those 50 years included a civil war and World War II, which killed at least 20 million people and devastated most of what had been built since the Revolution. The capital accumulation was used, in the first instance, to fight Hitler and thereafter to construct an immense military superstructure to defend against dangers from the U.S., or for its own military threat against Eastern Europe and China. Such efforts consumed staggering resources.

Basically the timing of the détente can be understood mainly by reference to the needs of Western capitalism, since the Soviets have for decades advocated peaceful coexistence. Nevertheless, there are dynamics within their own economic system which have in recent years created greater internal pressures, thereby setting the context for the successful Western economic penetration of the U.S.S.R.

### The Soviet Economic Crisis

The perennial complaint of Soviet managers has been the relatively low productivity of the Russian workers, a condition that has largely resisted their various exhortations and incentive efforts. From the mid-1960s the annual GNP growth rate, which was 6 percent between 1956 and 1966, began to fall to 5.5 percent between 1966 and 1970, 3.5 percent in 1971, and was reported to be less than 2 percent in 1972. The disastrous harvest of 1972 accounted for a good part of this decline but there were also production losses in chemicals, ferrous metals, and natural gas. Much of Russia's rapid growth of the 1950s and 1960s depended on a very large increase in the work force which leaped 27 million between 1950 and 1970. Now with a labor shortage, the U.S.S.R. is importing workers from North Korea, Bulgaria, and Finland.

And even though Soviet leadership recognized the problems in agriculture as serious, and his failures in this field proved an important factor in the downfall of Khrushchev, by 1965 the Soviets still allocated only 18 percent of the national budget to this critical sector. During the 1950s the Russians increased the land under production by 40 percent; 31 percent of the work force is still in the agricultural sector, but young farm workers continued to emigrate to the cities, and today the average Russian farm worker is 50 years old. It was therefore inevitable that there be a grain problem which directly affected meat production, and it was further compounded by weather factors which have been important in setting back national plans for years. In the last bad harvest in 1963 the Russians were forced to slaughter livestock for lack of feed, retarding meat consumption goals by many years. The Russians are also committed to grain deliveries to East Europe, a fact that places additional demands on output and strains on the entire economy. Progress was achieved between 1966 and 1970, but, thereafter, declined although the U.S.S.R. decided in 1970 to raise the agricultural sector's share of the budget to 35 percent by 1975.

In the consumer goods sector, without high priority for decades, the central planners had routinely allocated production quotas, and factories met them with drab, shoddy goods which, by the 1960s, were filling warehouses with mountains of unwanted products — the symbols of waste. The population preferred to put their increased wages, acquired in 1965 in the new money incentive plans, into the bank, and personal savings rose from 18.7 billion rubles in 1965 to 53.2 billion in 1971. There was a scarcity of those few desired goods produced and a substantial black market.

Over the past decades, the technicians, managers, teachers, professionals, bureaucrats, and intellectuals have grown into a substantial class of millions in the U.S.S.R. and Eastern Europe. These people, already privileged within the society, have deep-seated aspirations to attain what can only be described as an expanding, consumption-oriented, bourgeois life. There is much evidence that the "dissent" in the U.S.S.R. originates wholly in this class and centers on a consumption-oriented ideology. Its members' admiration for the U.S. is repeatedly evident as there is more contact between the managers and elites of the two countries. The top Russian rulers themselves who are also part of this same class now tend to frame comparisons of the societies in terms of consumption of commodities. This class and its ideology is the natural outcome of the manner in which the U.S.S.R. evolved over the past 50 years. It seems probable that since this class holds power in Russia the government will continue to respond to its needs — at the expense of the working class. The Western "concern" over the living conditions in East Europe, in turn, has always reflected its solicitude for its own class counterparts — the intellectuals, managers, and the middle class. It is from this class that the intellectual dissidents, the Solzhenitsyns and the Sakharovs. spring.

The Western press's discussions of economic "reform" in Eastern Europe always refer to the introduction of capitalist market techniques — including increased inequality as a labor incentive, greater profit motives, private investments, interest charges on capital, a market basis for production plans, advertising, and the like. These so-called "reforms," or new economic measures, were introduced in the Soviet and East European economies after 1965. As the failure and economic waste of the system of consumer production decisions and low productivity became evident, a group of technical economists led by Evsei Lieberman proposed the use of market choice and company profit to determine production in certain industries. A central planning agency would assign a predetermined "profit" as opposed to the former measure of a quantity of goods, and a percentage would go to the state as a tax and the rest would remain for use, at the discretion of the manager, for further investment, bonuses, or worker benefits. The Russian managers envisage that eventually any excess profit will stay with them as an additional production incentive. The Svetlana electronics combine's manager, for example, reported that he meets production quotas in terms of profits and on the basis of market demand, and "If there aren't enough sales contracts in my portfolio [for electronic goods] to achieve this, we will conclude contracts for guitar strings or something else."[18] More than 1,000 enterprises of this sort were operating by mid-1973 and they accounted for 12 percent of the sales of output and profits in the U.S.S.R. The Russians are now considering introducing a wholesale sector into the distribution system of consumer goods in the economy as well. The deputy chief of Gosplan in the U.S.S.R. also noted that "[t]he expansion of the production apparatus and the scale of production, the deepening social division of labor, the increasing complexity of economic relations . . . ," all required a change in the pricing policy.[19]

Although such "reforms" could hardly be described as having solved their crisis of productivity, the Russians made the decision in 1973 to expand their role in the economy. Earlier the U.S.S.R. had moved merely toward a greater dependence on more advanced technology, including computers, to implement its strict central planning, but there was clearly considerable debate on the topic and in mid-1973 the choice was made as the Party officially attacked the old "conservative" economists, which is to say the ideological ones, and opted for the new economic mathematicians and technicians. They chose to organize large new enterprises incorporating groups of factories on a principle similar to the large Western conglomerate corporations, and decentralize to the manager "questions concerning production and economic activities" and to dismantle several tiers of the central planning bureaucracy, yet the debate continued into 1974.[20]

### Eastern European Reforms

The other Eastern European governments introduced "reforms" similar to those in the Soviet Union and they had diverse consequences. Certain East European countries went much farther along this path than did the Russians. Hungary, in particular, exuberantly adopted the "new" economics and such policies, which were essentially the outcome of a search for greater productivity (within the context of the old work organization) and the expansion of a consumer society, created their own dynamics and reaction. Since 40 percent of Hungary's national income is from foreign trade, enterprises are permitted to engage in trade independently. These efforts have begun to have serious detrimental effects on the balance-of-payments. Moreover, the Hungarian bank has begun to use profit criteria rather than a central plan for investment loans. The establishment of market-oriented, profit-making companies has gone so far over the past five years that there has even been a left-wing reaction from students, academics, and even within the Party. The Russians, in addition, have leveled a rebuke at Budapest's tactics, although it may also be motivated by their differences over the onerous growing export of raw materials to Hungary for its burgeoning consumer industry. Within Hungary, students have attacked the "money-grubbing" and, as one Hungarian economist wrote, "What can the reaction of the workers be to the fact that luxury is often flaunted and that they must sometimes face the arrogance of the newly rich as well."[21] The workers, indeed, are being left out of the "bonuses" of the new enterprises and the government recently had to order the enterprises to raise wages by as high as 8 percent. The spirit of "enrichissez-vous" had advanced so far in five years' time that even the Party paper had to bemoan the fact that Party members "have had a chance to improve their personal financial situation," criticizing "the materialism and bourgeois selfishness" in Hungarian society.[22] Clearly the Party by 1972 had not fully resolved its position on these questions, allowing for some debate, as in Russia before June 1973, as to the propriety of the new trends.

The admiration of the Communist managers for the United States appears boundless. In Hungary and Rumania they seem to share with the West Europeans the naive and anti-materialist notion that American economic success in the world rests on some skill or "know-how" in business management. The Harvard Business School became the model for management institutes in both Hungary and Rumania, which use both its techniqu and texts. They have found it safer to apply literally all the capitalist techniques and precepts than to delegate, in their search for greater productivity, even limited decision-making power to the workers — making many Western capitalists look less reactionary by comparison.

In Poland, efforts such as these played an important role in creating the conditions that led to the workers' revolt in Gdansk and Szczecim in December 1970 to February 1971. Seemingly in the remote bureaucratic world of macro-economic decisions, the Polish leaders had decided to lower the price of consumer appliances for work incentives and export purposes, while at the same moment balance accounts by raising the prices of food by 30 percent. What followed was apparently a real shock to the entire Soviet bloc. The workers revolted, sacked the party headquarters, and demanded that the

government respond to their real needs. The government first
answered with force, shooting some workers in the street.
But rather quickly Gomulka was expelled, the leadership
changed, and the new head of the Party eventually felt compelled to meet with the workers at their work place and listen
to their grievances. They were not revolting for more consumer goods, and it was not their class that was demanding
more commodities, intellectual freedom, modern art, travel
rights, and the like. These workers demanded decision-making
in the factories, a living wage for food, safe working conditions, such elementary things as hot showers in the factory,
and decent housing. They protested the inequality in Poland
and even established communist workers' councils in Szczecim
for a time. In short, they attacked the distinctly nonsocialist
nature of Polish society.

There was doubtless no conspiracy among the rulers of
Poland to victimize the workers; there was only a profound
alienation from, if not indifference to, the actual conditions of
the working class. The extent was demonstrated by their failure even to try to explain their moves to the people. Engrossed
in their new "reforms," incentive theories, and policies that
had sharply reduced the workers' real income since the beginning of 1970, they simply took it for granted, as did their
counterparts around the world, that the workers had always
paid, and would continue to pay, the price for their economic
decisions. But the workers made a point in Poland, and if
they did not achieve their goals the government was forced
for a time to modify many of its "reforms." The point was
also made throughout the bloc, especially Russia, that a
greater emphasis would have to be placed on the problems of
the agricultural sector of the economy and at least adequate
food for the workers, if not political power.[23]

What will be the outcome of this emphasis on the so-
called "market choice" if the market is assigned the role of controlling prices and the allocation of production, and this market
remains highly stratified. Although in Russia the income inequality has been reduced since the Stalin era, economic
privileges for the managerial and professional classes increased
since Khrushchev's fall chiefly under the impact of the eco-

nomic "reforms." Will this mean that the new class, the group with the real spending power, will see that the workers produce useless luxury commodities while the real needs of the society are neglected and the working class's status continues to fall in the "workers' states"? Could the Soviet and East European economies become vulnerable to some of the crisis characteristics of the capitalist market economies? It may be that, in the short run, the measures taken in the U.S.S.R. and the rest of Eastern Europe may also lead to the same economic crises and contradictions, thereby further compounding rather than curing the economic ills from which the system is presently suffering. For the new class dynamics, coupled with the leaders' own sense of failure over the existing operations, can certainly lead in this direction.[24]

### Expanded Relations with the West

The congruence of circumstances — Soviet desires and needs along with the crisis of capitalism — meant that the times were opportune for new relations with the West, particularly the United States. New arrangements could at once relieve pressures on Moscow for protracted high military expenditures as well as provide a leap forward in the expansion of the consumer sector.

Loans and trade from the Western states can accelerate the development of natural resources and shortcut the accumulation of capital. The Russians plan to import finished goods, factories, and, like the Japanese, technology. It is cheaper for them both in time and resources to pay for the latter with royalties and license fees, and for the American corporations it is a sheer bonus. To improve the consumer sector means considerably more than a greater supply of commodities. The infrastructure itself is underdeveloped. The Russians are building huge truck factories for the distribution system, and they have indicated to the Americans that they also need to buy railroad rolling stock.

In order to purchase their needs in the West, the Russians and the East Europeans need hard, convertible currencies.

There are today several means that they have to acquire them that did not exist a number of years ago. Gold stocks are an obvious source, If the price of gold maintains anything like its present value. Russian gold reserves have more than quadrupled in a few years. Another obvious possibility, of course, is to borrow, and as we have seen in earlier chapters, both private and government bankers in the West are eager to satisfy them on this score. It has clearly been a borrower's market since 1971, although with the restrictions of credit throughout the capitalist world the situation may alter sharply. Nevertheless, the Eastern governments will remain among the safest risks available to Western bankers.

While the Soviets are gambling that the debt service problem will be less costly than inflation, it will be substantial. Michael Kaser of Oxford University estimated in 1973 that debt service absorbed 22 percent of export earnings and that by 1980 the U.S.S.R. would have a foreign debt of roughly $29 billion and that service payments would absorb one-half of their export earnings. Thereafter the developed natural resources would shift the balance in their direction.[25] Of course these projections, like all such, are hypothetical in the extreme. Moreover, the contracted sale of up to an estimated $45 billion over 25 years in Siberian natural gas ties the revenue to purchases of American goods, even after the repayment of the original loans.

A number of the Eastern governments are also encouraging foreign private investment, including equity ownership up to 49 percent in some countries. Other means of earning currencies available to the East Europeans are joint ventures with Western capitalists in third countries, or their own direct investment abroad. The Hungarian companies have taken the lead in such joint ventures, primarily in the marketing of Hungarian products, but they also have a 30 percent interest in a British medical supply corporation. The Poles and Austrians have a joint construction venture in Greece. Among the direct investments by East European companies abroad are a Rumanian tractor assembly plant in Saskatchewan, Canada; Polish and Hungarian companies extract phosphate and potassium respectively in Canada; a Hungarian corporation makes miniature batteries in England; a Rumanian company operates a chain of restaurants in Germany; Polish and East German construction companies are building hotels in Western Europe; the Russians own a chain of gas stations in England and Belgium, a refinery in Brazil and Belgium, an auto assembly plant in Belgium; and they are planning to build an assembly plant in Colombia for their Yak 40 airplane to reach the Latin American market — to cite a few examples of an expanding trend. Despite what some believed would be ideological barriers to manufacturing on a large scale in capitalist countries, one Communist commercial attaché made it plain that "Our businessmen and Government officials are very practical in these matters. So long as a project makes a good profit, then there is nothing to stop us."[26]

Banking abroad has also been a profitable venture for the U.S.S.R. It has four banks operating in London, Paris, Zurich, and Frankfurt, with branches in Singapore and Beirut. They raise Eurodollar loans for export industries and projects abroad and are engaged in overall Eurodollar trading. "The Soviet bankers we know are good. They're conservative people. Don't kid yourself, they worry as much as we do about the stability of the dollar," was the estimate of one Western diplomat.[27] The Russians have also participated with Western banks in financing such projects in third countries as a Brazilian utility corporation, and its state insurance company participates in a wide range of insurance programs with Western firms, including a small share of reinsurance of U.S. government insurance (OPIC) against expropriation.

Finally, another incentive for better economic ties with the West is the less than satisfactory relations within the Council for Mutual Economic Assistance (COMECON), the East European common market organization. The "Soviet Bloc," according to the well informed, is little more than a cliché, and not a descriptive term of the economic relations between the Communist states. In many regards COMECON has become an economic liability for the U.S.S.R., especially recently in supplying raw materials, including oil at considerably less than they could get in the West, and receiving inferior manufactured goods in return. It has begun to encourage the COMECON states to get a greater share of their oil from the Arab nations. The same is true of their commitments to supply grain and other basic materials. The East European states, on the other hand, tend to reserve their best products for their trade with the West and to dump their shoddier goods on their protected market in the U.S.S.R. Within COMECON all trade is bilateral and negotiated in advance. Basically, their dependence on Soviet raw materials and markets, for which there is no foreseeable alternative under any political regime, makes it primarily of interest to the East European states to preserve.

Going considerably beyond borrowing funds on the private capital markets of the world, Rumania joined the IMF and World Bank in September 1972, and Hungary is expected to follow.[28] This should eventually require some important adjustments from these two states or the IMF, for, as we know, the IMF is much more than a bank; rather, it is an integrative mechanism of world capitalism, touching directly on the formulation of government economic policies. Utilizing the drawing rights and "services" of the Fund and Bank, the only reason for their joining them, could require significant alterations of existing Hungarian and Rumanian economic practices to conform to capitalist norms.

Politics is not a criterion for aid and trade with the Third World either. The sole demand is rather a policy of détente and peaceful coexistence on the part of the varying regimes. Under these circumstances, Russia's dual role as a state operating in the world of *realpolitik* and as an ideological mecca for the world Communist parties increasingly subverts revolutionary struggles around the world. Not only do the Russians counsel moderation in political tactics, as they always have, but their new economic ties with repressive regimes throughout the world strengthens these regimes materially. Aid and trade with Brazil, with Greece, with Spain, the Philippines, *et al*, can be only of the most marginal economic benefit to the U.S.S.R., but of significant value to the recipients. One of the implications was underlined when Poland helped break the miners' strike in Spain by supplying shipments of coal to the Franco regime in 1970.[29]

But it is, of course, Indochina where the real contradiction is most evident. The Soviet Union has benefited enormously from the Vietnamese struggle, and it owes the Vietnamese a colossal debt. Not only did Vietnam greatly diminish the U.S. capacity to pursue the arms race with the U.S.S.R. for one decade, but it was a crucial factor in creating the crisis in capitalism that led the American ruling class to push strongly for the détente. To make deals with the U.S. only to attain greater consumption of commodities, when Russia was under no threat and capitalism was facing severe internal crises, and while the U.S. was employing ever-escalating brutality in Indochina, was indeed a rank betrayal of the Vietnamese.

Time and again the Soviet's desire not to aggravate relations with the U.S. caused it to counsel national revolutionary movements to submerge their grievances in the interest of "international socialism" and the "security of the workers state." The discipline of the world Communist parties was often sufficient to follow this direction. It may be different when the needs are patently no longer security but instead a greater consumption of commodities. It is irrelevant to try to understand the Russian policy from the point of view of their own national security or even their estimate of an uneven struggle, for objectively its counsel has consistently served the interest of counterrevolution.

### The China Perspective

Although there had been considerable pressure from an important sector of the ruling class for some years to change American policy toward China, essentially for the same reasons that they advocated a shift with the U.S.S.R., it was, even more in China than the U.S.S.R., a fortuitous congruence of political and economic needs that dictated a revision in American policy between 1969 and 1971. As Assistant Secretary of State for East Asia Marshall Green pointed out, "it is hardly conceivable that this evolution in our relationship could have occurred at the time of the Great Leap Forward . . . or during the period of the subsequent Cultural Revolution in China. In other words, it would have been very difficult for these changes to have come about before 1969."[30] Yet as early as 1968 Nixon prepared an undelivered speech outlining his ideas on a détente. Clearly, these views did not originate with him but had been articulated through prolonged consultation with the men of power and influence in the Republican party, men to whom a shift in policy toward both Communist powers was mandatory. What undoubtedly appealed to Nixon was less the economics involved than the political strategy of buying off the great powers in order to achieve military victory in Vietnam, a strategy many probably believed would be an ultimate counterinsurgency weapon everywhere. It is probable that Nixon as a Republican had considerably more freedom politically to carry out these policies, but doubtless Humphrey would also have done the same, even if more cautiously, because a quarantine of China was demonstrably no longer in the interest of anyone with power.

The timing of the announcement of a trip to China was politically spectacular. The economic pressures in the summer of 1971 were intense from all quarters and had begun to spill over into political demands for total withdrawal from Vietnam. With one stroke Nixon was able to introduce the uninformed to the new relations with China, preparation for which had been under way for more than two years, with its unknown, but potentially great, market for American production, and to alleviate the pressure to withdraw from Vietnam with the tantalizing hint that perhaps the Chinese and Russians could end the war while allowing the U.S. to maintain a neo-colonial presence in the area. The negative repercussions of the new China policy with Japan were, in fact, only tangential. The economic conflict with that Asian power was a reality of the most fundamental sort and could not be papered over with security treaties that supposedly were shaken by the President's visit to China. The move only accelerated the shift within the Japanese ruling class toward negotiating their own profitable accommodation with China. Premier Sato clearly felt betrayed, for Japan's political policy toward China, which handicapped expanded trade relations, was in response to American pressure, and suddenly, without consultation, the U.S. was engaged in making its own separate accords while it was also restricting Japanese trade. Such organizations as SEATO had in fact already been reoriented by the so-called Nixon Doctrine, which presupposed that the great Communist powers would remain aloof while the U.S. aided the other nations to counter insurgency within their own borders. Nevertheless, such major shifts in policy did weaken the foundations of U.S. alliances in Asia but not so seriously as to offset the gains it expected from its new relations with China.

The promise of new economic relations with China for Western capitalism is considerably smaller than that offered by the U.S.S.R. After the U.S. eliminated the political restraints to expanded trade in 1971, China remained what Marshall Green called "one of the most conservative states in international financial dealings."[31] By this he meant that China, uniquely in the world, was virtually debt free and insisted on balanced trade or paying in cash or bartered goods. Given the nature of Chinese exports, this posed a serious obstacle to anything more than limited sales to the coveted China market. By the end of 1972 only Boeing, RCA, and the wheat growers had benefited substantially from the new trade relations. For the few banks that have access to China, usually only one per nation, the prospects for profit are considerably greater than in the U.S.S.R., where the competition has virtually eliminated the profit margin.

In January 1973 the Chinese indicated that they would waive this ideological barrier to pay interest and indeed accept a disguised form of interest in order to purchase their major requirements. While this new position whetted the appetite of additional industries and banks and may lead to sales of oil refineries, mining machinery, and transport equipment, it soon became clear that the bulk of Chinese purchases would be with Japanese corporations for industrial supplies and with Australia and Canada for agricultural needs. The Europeans are actively trying to expand their trade relations, and the U.S.

government in early 1973 set up an intermediary committee of leading businessmen to deal with the Chinese purchasing agencies and to promote competitively American trade. Hostility between European, Japanese, and American rivals was aroused by early 1972 when RCA sold a communications network to China that the Europeans and Japanese had earlier wanted to sell but were prevented by the U.S. government's insisting it was strategic goods. From that time on the China market has become one of competitive struggle between the various Western and Japanese capitalists. Trade with the U.S. grew from zero in 1970 to over $600 million in 1973, but it is far less likely to expand in the manner of Soviet trade.

### Chinese Interests

A far greater surprise to the world than the U.S.-Soviet détente, or even the U.S. desire to change its policy toward China, was the Chinese receptivity. We can only surmise what led to this apparent about-face in their foreign policy, including their unwillingness to terminate contacts with the U.S. even during the most brutal escalation of the Vietnam war during 1972 — to the point of such peripheral but symbolic gestures of cynically allowing visiting Chinese delegations to be photographed amicably with Nixon while American planes destroyed Vietnamese cities. The forces probably causing the shift in Chinese policy would seem different from those in the U.S.S.R. and to reflect three major considerations: security, economic needs, and the long-standing aspiration to liberate the millions of Chinese in Taiwan.

The primary security consideration that has, ostensibly, weighed ever more heavily on their calculations over the past decade has been the growing tension with the U.S.S.R. The Chinese have apparently explained to their own people that policy toward the U.S. changed because of the growing danger from the Russians, likening it to the joint effort with Chiang Kai-Shek to defeat the Japanese during World War II. The economic motivations are in part an outgrowth of this fear for their security. The threat of war with Russia probably prompted

Chinese desire to accelerate economic development in certain lagging sectors, undoubtedly affected by the great social upheaval of the Cultural Revolution. But the Chinese social matrix and internal dynamics are in marked contrast to the Russian, and their reasons for seeking new relations with the capitalist states are quite different. There is, seemingly, no interest in establishing a consumer industry to meet the needs of a new class or as an incentive for production, or an inequitable stratified society. On the contrary, China, a considerably poorer nation, in great part destroyed the emerging privileges of the managerial class during the Cultural Revolution and relies much more on political and ideological education and the evidence of equality as a motivating force. Equality, besides being a desirable social goal ideologically, has an economic rationale of importance for a poor society. As the Chinese explained it to one Western observer, their aim was not to create new and peripheral demand by differentiating groups with unequal incomes, nor would they produce for the market items which could not be consumed by all. And one would suspect that it is easier to elicit the motivation and cooperation of the people for the huge task of economic development if equality is apparent rather than if the workers and peasants see an obvious privileged class being constructed above them and with the production incentives exactly the same as in Western capitalist states.

Since the Chinese do not aim at an expanded consumer goods industry, at least at this stage, the China market is structurally of a different composition and promise than the Russian for Western capitalists. Their focus is on power complexes, steel mills, refineries, and transportation equipment intended to faci-facilitate distribution. And most of their contacts are with the Japanese.[32]

While the effects of the Cultural Revolution are being moderated, although apparently not reversed, the Chinese, like the Russians, have divorced ideology from international state relations and have fully accepted the rules of *realpolitik*. In opening diplomatic ties with fascist regimes around the world, to the extent of economic aid, they have not restricted their contacts to simply correct formal relations but have lavished effusive praise on the Shah of Iran, the King of Ethiopia, and the governments of Ceylon and Pakistan, and others of similar character. Any understandings they may have had with the Americans regarding the liberation of Taiwan were not quickly forthcoming, other than their replacement in international bodies like the U.N., and the Americans doubtless are holding the future of Taiwan as a trump card in future political negotiations.

## Conclusion

The Soviet bloc and China, while appearing potentially to hold in their hands the only "life-buoy" for a sinking capitalist system, have, in fact, been permitted to join the society too late. What will occur if the present uniform credit policies lead to the expected "slowdown" or recession of the economies throughout Europe, North America, and Japan? What will happen to the oil shortage, and the U.S. interest in the Siberian reserves? What can they do if stagnation and unemployment overwhelm the capitalist states, and the overexpansion of manufacturing in the Third World compound, with the fall in demand for raw materials, the crises in these areas? Can the Soviet bloc provide the escape when the political tensions, competitive devaluations, tariffs, and trade blocs ensue? Could the Soviet and Chinese markets save the situation if the biggest markets collapse simultaneously for all? Will the "secure" but low profit loans to Russia save the banks forced into default? Merely to raise the questions shows how preposterous an affirmative answer would be.

The industrial capitalist states seek a supplementary market in the U.S.S.R. and China, but their primary market remains in Western Europe, North America, and Japan. And the lure of Soviet raw materials is generated by the current booming economy that makes their shortage the felt need of the system. The interest in new sources will diminish rapidly if there is a glut from falling demand. The position of banks throughout the world is already too perilous to gain any compensating security in loans to the Communist states.

The crises and contradictions that have in fact driven the U.S. to seek a "new frontier" with the centrally planned economies are now too advanced and the markets of the U.S.S.R., Eastern Europe, and China too limited at this stage in history to compensate for the conflict, potentially explosive social tensions, and political rivalries among the capitalist states. Thus, regardless of the intentions of all the world's political and corporate leaders, the new role of the U.S.S.R. and China in the capitalist world economy has come too late to salvage it.

# CONCLUSION

The essence of world capitalism today remains its contradictions and vulnerability, and this overriding reality is now the permanent, fundamental condition of the system. Its fragility is enhanced by the congruence of circumstances that have irreversibly evolved over the recent years, and which I have elaborated throughout this book. They include the coordination of the "business cycles" of the industrial states, the massive and new concentration of corporate decision-making power that can — and will — accelerate any crisis and more rapidly spread it around the globe, and the perilous situation in an international credit structure that involves unprecedented risks on the part of the largest banks. These factors, in turn, are compounded by the intensifying trade conflict on the part of the industrial states acting as representatives for warring corporate interests, and the sharpening of the old struggle for markets and raw materials. And it is clear that all the industrial "powers" are susceptible to the same crises, and, in fact, like the giant corporations, their domestic crises have the greatest impact on the rest of the world as each state seeks solutions to its internal dilemmas outside its own borders. And within these industrial nations there is intensifying class conflict as a reactivated working class escalates its demands on the social system. All concepts of monopolization and omnipotent corporations, which allege their strength and stability, are exaggerated, for the entire system is torn by warring competition and is very much in the stage of national capitalism.

In the Third World, worsening economic conditions offer little hope of a compensating market for the developed economies, and the search for cheap labor there only heightens the social conflicts in the industrial countries and can only be a temporary expedient. While war in the Third World, against Korea and Indochina, did prevent depression in the industrial economies, it also created its own disintegrating effect on the system. This very disintegration, in fact, opened the doors to the U.S.S.R. and China to have a greater role in the world capitalist economy. But as I noted in Chapter Six, the structural problems were already too grave for the eagerly wooed new market in the centrally planned economies to have a significant offsetting effect for the crisis in the world system.

Throughout these chapters a point that emerges again and again is the impersonal nature of the world capitalist system. The bankers know the risks, but are compelled to continue to take them; the investing corporate managers operate on the basis of short-term profit, even in contradiction to their long-term requirements; governments consistently introduce orthodox economic measures which lead to new crises; and "development" authorities in the Third World introduce policies that undermine development. Capitalism in this systemic, compulsive sense is the origin of the current malaise around the globe, and it allows for no reform. It is less the acts of perverse men than the operation of the system which has not changed in fundamentals and which inexorably will continue to reach into the lives of the people in all corners of the world and destroy through war, repression, and exploitation until the system itself is destroyed. Yet the operations of the capitalist system can and will engineer its own demise. But this fact alone will scarcely suffice, for the collapse may also end in world war or fascism. The social movement of resistance that can potentially transform that collapse into a new and better society must come from the political struggle of the working class — from those for whom there is no other exit from oppression and exploitation. A sense of moral outrage over the crimes against others, while a very real and salutary sentiment, is insufficient to mobilize many for the prolonged struggle necessary for social change. This is, of course, why all change of economic and social systems must be class-based and can never rest on men of "goodwill," whether liberal or radical. But one cannot be neutral toward capitalism as a system and oppose this or that aspect of it. Given the nature of decision-making and the consistent, impersonal, and fundamentally destructive compulsions of capitalist operations, there is no way, except through self-deception, to "work within the system" to reform or modify it. Reformism is as utopian, if not as inspiring, as the most extreme anarchist dream. It cultivates the illusion of opposition while really falling prey to an ideology that has crippled American resistance for generations.

It is a time of crisis, as always, but also, once more, a time of hope for revolutionary change as a congruence of factors in the world economy merge. The exact details of future developments cannot be predicted, but the dynamics at play are clear. For today the social dynamics of industrial capitalism, particularly in Western Europe, are such that a severe recession may lead to class conflict of a most intense sort. The class basis of society never changes because the standard of living rises or the consumption of commodities is expanded. It is encountered everywhere in the organization of work and of society. The new worker demands prove that their militancy and potential revolutionary motivations do not rest simply on their immediate consumption of commodities but on the social relations of exploitation, as well as their vulnerability to shifts in the economy. A developing focal point of conflict is now found in most industrial nations among relatively highly paid unskilled and skilled workers.

As the economic system breaks down further and factories close or masses of workers are laid off, this current political situation is potentially explosive. There is manifestly a different political environment among the workers of Europe than less than a decade ago, and a crisis in capitalism may yet meet an entirely different political response. The capitalists themselves understand this, and for this reason there will be considerable conflict between the capitalist states (in trade war and the like) to try to minimize the internal political effect by forcing other nations to absorb the shock.

A struggle to transform an industrial capitalist nation to a socialist one would scarcely be a peaceful occurrence. There has been general confidence among those who wield power that their class has unchallenged control of the European and North American societies, allowing for a moderate response to class conflict and toleration of social critics. But once that ruling class feels really threatened in the industrial states, it will react with whatever means available, as it has in the past, to preserve its position of power.

One cannot predict where, when, or how forces of resistance in the Third World will challenge both imperialist domination and local ruling cliques. There is an intimate link between the events in the industrial and the preindustrial regions. If the past decade has been one of reactionary victory over large areas, the struggle in Indochina has substantially weakened the foundations of the global system, making it more difficult for it to confront or prevail over subsequent crises wherever they may occur. Social movements can be aided but they cannot be initiated or terminated externally; they can be suppressed but they cannot be eradicated as long as the objective circumstances of exploitation remain. Accords among states are irrelevant to the social dynamics of resistance.

Yet the danger remains. In periods of falling or stagnating economic activity, the U.S. in the past has stimulated its economy by responding to constantly available social crisis in the Third World by military intervention. But the social context never remains static, and each future situation must face a new arrangement of forces everywhere and so the same response will meet a different constellation of circumstances that can lead to a decisively different outcome.

The world economy in the 1970s is one of unshakable constancy in the fundamental motivations of capitalist behavior operating in a world of ceaseless change and interaction of dynamic forces. By tracing the various factors and pointing to their congruence, the evolving crisis becomes more comprehensible, but the exact details of the evolution cannot be foreseen. The forces in operation are economic, political, and social — the capitalists themselves in the immensely powerful corporations and banks each pursue their individual needs, while their governments try to create order out of the chaos with their destabilizing, counterproductive, orthodox monetary and fiscal policies. These forces, in turn, stimulate political struggles within and between the states, and unanticipated crises like the war in the Mideast further expose and accelerate other fragile conditions. Finally, and most importantly for those who desire a world different from the capitalist barbarism of the past and present, there is the potential social movement of the working class in the industrial world whose actions, in response, could transform the social system. One cannot predict the outcome; one can only comprehend the forces of crisis. And the crises of world capitalism are fraught both with danger and with the hope of change.

# NOTES

*I have tried to keep the footnotes to a minimum — to identify quotations and specific facts. I am, of course, indebted to a vast body of additional literature that I have not been able to cite in the notes. In all quotations the first reference of the note identifies the quotation. The references that follow refer to facts cited since the previous note.*

### Introduction

1. Paul Mattick, *Marx and Keynes: The Limits of the Mixed Economy* (Boston, 1969), 70.

### Chapter One

1. Eliot Janeway, *The Economics of Crisis: War, Politics, and the Dollar* (New York, 1968), 254-61; Maurice Flamant and Jeanne Singer-Kerel, *Modern Economic Crises* (London, 1970), 92-104.
2. *OECD Observer*, April 1964, 8-11; United Nations, Economic Commission for Europe, *Economic Survey of Europe in 1966* (Geneva, 1967), 1; *U.S. News and World Report*, February 14, 1958, 43-46.
3. *Fortune*, July 1966, 15-16, 22; *Federal Reserve Bulletin*, April 1970, 320; First National City Bank, *Monthly Economic Letter*, September 1971, 10.
4. *Fortune*, May 1971, 163. See also *Forbes*, December 1, 1970, 20; *Journal of Commerce*, January 25, 1972, 1.
5. Quoted in *Wall Street Journal*, November 13, 1970. See also First National City Bank, *Monthly Economic Letter*, March 1970; *Le Monde* (weekly English selection), June 10, 1970; *Economist*, April 10, 1971, 67; *Business Week*, May 15, 1971, 16-17; *Wall Street Journal*, October 14, 1970; *New York Times*, November 26, 1970.
6. *Wall Street Journal*, June 18, 1971. See also *ibid.*, November 13, 1970; First National City Bank, *Monthly Economic Letter*, October 1971, 12.
7. *Wall Street Journal*, February 17, 1971; *Business Week*, March 13, 1971, 88-89; *Wall Street Journal*, April 7, 1971.
8. Quoted in *Wall Street Journal*, May 7, 1971. See also *New York Times*, April 19, 1971.
9. Quoted in *Wall Street Journal*, May 11, 1971.
10. Quoted in *International Herald Tribune*, June 5-6, 1971. See also *ibid.*, June 26-27, 1971, June 28, 1971; *New York Times*, July 27, 1971; *Business Week*, August 21, 1971, 27; First National City Bank, *Monthly Economic Letter*, March 1970.
11. Quoted by J. Robert Schaetzel, "A Dialogue of the Deaf Across the

Atlantic," *Fortune*, November 1972, 149.

12. Quoted in *Business Week*, August 7, 1971, 21, 19.

13. Quoted in *International Herald Tribune*, September 18-19, 1971. See also *Le Monde*, September 14, 1971; *Business Week*, August 21, 1971, 21-27; *Federal Reserve Bulletin*, April 1970, 322; *Business Week*, December 12, 1970, 63; *Wall Street Journal*, August 13, 1971.

14. Quoted in *International Herald Tribune*, September 18-19, 1971. See also *Business Week*, October 23, 1971, 44; *New York Times*, November 3, 1971; *International Herald Tribune*, November 9, 1971.

15. *Wall Street Journal*, November 26, 1971; December 10, 1971; *International Herald Tribune*, November 12, 13-14, 1971, December 21, 1971; *New York Times*, November 9, 1971; *Business Week*, January 8, 1972, 17; United Nations, Department of Economic and Social Affairs, *World Economic Survey 1971: Current Economic Developments* (New York, 1972), 4.

16. *Le Monde*, January 18, 1972.

17. Quoted in *Wall Street Journal*, January 11, 1972. See also *ibid.*, January 10, 1972; *Business Week*, January 15, 1972, 19-20.

18. Quoted in *Business Week*, January 29, 1972, 52-53.

19. Quoted in *Business Week*, December 25, 1971, 37.

20. Quoted in *Wall Street Journal*, February 17, 1972.

21. Eldridge Haynes, "What U.S. Bankers Should Know About the USSR," *The Bankers Magazine* (Boston), Summer 1972, 31. See also *Journal of Commerce*, January 25, 1972; *Washington Post*, January 20, 1972; Federal Reserve Bank of New York, *Monthly Review*, May 1972, 113.

22. Quoted in *New York Times*, January 21, 1973. See also *New York Times*, December 3, 1972; Victor R. Farhi, "Stop and Go Again," *Bankers Magazine*, Winter, 1973, 95; *Business Week*, May 6, 1972, 35.

23. First National City Bank, *Monthly Economic Letter*, December 1971, 12.

24. Quoted in *Business Week*, April 21, 1973, 40.

25. Quoted in *International Herald Tribune*, July 18, 1973. See also *ibid.*, May 22, 1973; May 31, 1973; *Le Monde*, May 11, 1973.

Chapter Two

1. U.S. Senate, Committee on the Judiciary, *Hearings: Economic Concentration, Federal Trade Commission Staff Report*, 91:1 (Washington, 1969), 161, 163. See also Betty L. Barker, "U.S.

Foreign Trade Associated with U.S. Multinational Companies," *Survey of Current Business*, December 1972, 22; Raymond Vernon, *Manager in the International Economy* (Englewood Cliffs, New Jersey, 1968), 167-69; Henry P. Mueller, "How to Borrow Abroad from a U.S. Bank," *Journal of Commercial Bank Lending*, March 1973, 34-36; Sanford Rose, "Multinational Corporations in a Tough New World," *Fortune*, August 1973, 414; United Nations, Department of Economic and Social Affairs, *World Economic Survey 1971: Current Economic Developments* (New York, 1972), 96; *Fortune*, May 1972, 185-87; George Modelski, "Multinational Business," *International Studies Quarterly*, December 1972, 409.

2. Quoted in *Business Week*, December 19, 1970, 59. See also First National City Bank, *Monthly Economic Letter*, October 1971, 11.

3. Modelski, "Multinational Business," 429; U. S. Senate, Committee on Finance, Subcommittee on International Trade, *Hearings: Multinational Corporations*, 93: 1, February-March, 1973 (Washington, 1973) 403; *Wall Street Journal*, January 13, 1972; *Business Week*, July 7, 1973, 56; J. Robert Schaetzel, "A Dialogue of the Deaf Across the Atlantic," *Fortune*, November 1972, 150; *Business Week*, September 25, 1971, 101; Louis Turner, *Invisible Empires: Multinational Companies in the Modern World* (New York, 1970), 23.

4. *Industry Week*, July 31, 1972, 15-16; Jonathan Galloway, "The Military Industrial Linkages of U.S.-Based Multinational Corporation," *International Studies Quarterly*, December 1972, 500-03; Lawrence B. Krause, "The International Economic System and the Multinational Corporation," *The Annals*, September 1972, 96; *Survey of Current Business*, November 1972, 32, 21; October 1973, 6-8; *Wall Street Journal*, November 1, 1973; *Business Week*, January 12, 1974, 53.

5. Judd Polk, *et al.*, *U.S. Production Abroad and the Balance of Payments* (NICB, nd), 73. See also James R. Piper, Jr., "How Firms Evaluate Foreign Investment Opportunities," *M.S.U. Business Topics*, Summer 1971, 11-20.

6. *Business Week*, September 4, 1971, 30.

7. *Business Abroad*, August 1970, 27. See also *Le Monde* (weekly English selection), July 1, 1970; *Vision*, June 1972, 38; Turner, *Invisible Empire*, 88; *Business Week*, January 13, 1973, 34.

8. Lee Charles Nehrt, ed., *International Finance for Multinational Business* (Scranton, 1972), 796; United Nations, Economic Commission for Europe, *Economic Bulletin for Europe*, 19:1 (Geneva, 1967),

61-67; *Wall Street Journal,* April 18, 1973; United Nations, Economic Commission for Europe, *European Economy From the 1950s to the 1970s* (New York, 1972); Wolfgang Pohle, "Germany Copes with Foreign Investment," *Columbia Journal of World Business,* September 1970, 33-38; Turner, *Invisible Empires,* 46; *Business Week,* October 21, 1972, 24.

9. Quoted in *Wall Street Journal,* May 26, 1972.

10. *Ibid.; New York Times,* January 17, 1973; *Business Week,* October 7, 1972, 52, 62.

11. *New York Times,* July 29, 1971; Ferdinand Ricardi, "Rey Commission's Final Report," *Le Monde* (weekly English selection), July 1, 1970; Phillip Cateora, "The Multinational Enterprise and Nationalism," *M.S.U. Business Topics,* Summer, 1971, 50; Schaetzel, "A Dialogue of the Deaf," 148-54.

12. *Commerce Today,* November 27, 1972, 38. See also Turner, *Invisible Empires,* 104; Vernon, *Manager in the International Economy,* 171-78; Nehrt, *International Finance,* 817; Julius Friedman and Leonard Lupo, "U.S. Direct Investment Abroad in 1971," *Survey of Current Business,* November 1972, 21-35.

13. U.S. Senate, Committee on Finance, *Hearings: Foreign Trade,* 92:1, May 19-21, 1971 (Washington, 1971), 88-89; Richard B. DuBoff and Edward S. Herman, "Corporate Dollars and Foreign Policy," *Commonweal,* April 21, 1972, 159-73.

14. Quoted in *International Herald Tribune,* May 6-7, 1972.

15. Quoted in *Wall Street Journal,* January 8, 1973. See also Wolfgang G. Friedman and Jean-Pierre Beguin, *Joint International Business Ventures in Developing Countries* (New York, 1971), 337, 369-70.

16. Quoted in *Business Week,* June 30, 1973, 63. See also *New York Times,* December 10, 1971; *Wall Street Journal,* April 10, 1973; U.S. Senate, Committee on Foreign Relations, *Hearings: Multinational Corporations and United States Foreign Policy,* 93:1, July 18-August 1, 1973 (Washington, 1973), 318, 389-90.

17. Quoted in *Wall Street Journal,* June 18, 1971. See also U.S. Senate, Committee on Finance, Subcommittee on International Trade, *Hearings: Multinational Corporations,* 25; Krause, "The International Economic System," 95; Modelski, "Multinational Business," 410-14; Barker, "U.S. Foreign Trade," 21; United Nations, Economic Commission for Europe, *The European Economy From the 1950s to the 1970s,* 61.

18. U.S. Senate, Committee on Finance, Subcommittee on International Trade, *Hearings: Foreign Trade,* 92:1, May 17-21, 1971 (Washington, 1971), 35. See also Harold B. Malmgren, "Coming Trade Wars?

(Neo-Mercantilism and Foreign Policy)," *Foreign Policy*, Winter 1970-71, 115-43; *New York Times*, January 28, 1973.

19. Quoted in *Wall Street Journal*, April 24, 1972. See also U.S. Senate, Committee on Finance, *Hearings: Foreign Trade*, 92:1, 253; *Wall Street Journal*, April 9, 1973; *Commerce Today*, December 25, 1972, 34-35; *Commerce Today*, November 13, 1972, 38-40.

20. Quoted in *Wall Street Journal*, April 24, 1972.

21. Schaetzel, "A Dialogue of the Deaf," 153.

22. *Business Week*, January 20, 1973, 32.

23. Schaetzel, "A Dialogue of the Deaf," 150. See also *New York Times*, March 12, 1972; *Business Week*, December 16, 1972, 38; *International Herald Tribune*, June 28, 1973; *Business Week*, January 20, 1973, 32; *Wall Street Journal*, February 1, 1973; *International Herald Tribune*, October 16-17, 1971; *New York Times*, September 24, 1972.

### Chapter Three

1. U.S. Congress, Joint Economic Committee, Subcommittee on Economic Policy, *Hearings: A Foreign Economic Policy for the 1970s*, 91:2, September-October 1970 (Washington, 1970) Pt. 5, 1067.

2. *The Economist*, September 14, 1957, 843-44. See also "Transatlantic Investment and the Balance of Payments," *Law and Contemporary Problems*, Winter 1969.

3. George Humphrey to Joseph Dodge, September 17, 1958, Joseph Dodge Papers, Miscellaneous Files, Box 1, Detroit Public Library.

4. *Survey of Current Business*, January 1966, 18. See also *ibid.*, February 1961, 16-19; *ibid.*, September 1961, 24; *ibid.*, August 1961, 21; Fred Klopstock, "Euromarkets and the Balance of Payments," *Law and Contemporary Problems*, Winter, 1969, 157-59.

5. Frances Bator, "The Political Economics of International Money," *Foreign Affairs*, October 1968, 57; Cora Sheplar and Leonhard Campbell, "United States Defense Expenditures Abroad," *Survey of Current Business*, December 1969, 40-47.

6. *International Herald Tribune*, August 16, 1973; *New York Times*, February 18, 20, 1973; *Wall Street Journal*, December 28, 1971, January 10, 1972.

7. *New York Times*, April 28, 1971. See also *Business Week*, September 25, 1971, 94-96; *Le Monde*, June 22, 1971; Lee Charles Nehrt, ed., *International Finance and Multinational Business* (Scranton, 1972), 426.

8. Henry P. Mueller, "Sighting in on International Lending," *Journal*

*of Commercial Bank Lending,* November 1972, 2.

9. *U. S. News and World Report,* December 4, 1972, 66. See also Paul Einzig, *The Eurodollar System* (London, 1970), 70; *Bankers Monthly,* December 15, 1972, 25; *Business Week,* September 15, 1973, 106; *Wall Street Journal,* April 19, 1973; Donald Mandich, "International Loans: Profit Center or Loss Leader?" *Journal of Commercial Bank Lending,* September 1972, 43; *Survey of Current Business,* December 1972, 36, 40; *ibid.,* August 1973, 22.

10. Merwin H. Waterman, "Capital Sources for Multi-National Companies," in Nehrt, ed., *International Finance,* 548. See also Einzig, *Eurodollar System,* 29.

11. Quoted in *Business Week,* October 7, 1972, 62.

12. Quoted in *Wall Street Journal,* November 24, 1972. See also Einzig, *Eurodollar System,* 66-67.

13. A. Robert Abboud, "Eurodollars in Today's World Market," in Nehrt, ed., *International Finance,* 414. See also *The Bankers Magazine,* Winter 1973, 91; *Wall Street Journal,* November 24, 1972; Einzig, *Eurodollar System,* 65; Abboud, "Eurodollars," 416.

14. Abboud, "Eurodollars," 411.

15. *Fortune,* December 1966, 93.

16. *Ibid.,* 94. See also *Economist,* October 22, 1966, 394-95.

17. Mueller, "Sighting in on International Lending," 11.

18. *Ibid.,* 10.

19. *The Bankers Magazine,* Winter, 1973, 91. See also *Wall Street Journal,* November 24, 1972.

20. Quoted in *Wall Street Journal,* April 3, 1973. See also *International Herald Tribune,* August 3, 1973.

21. Quoted in *Business Week,* September 15, 1973, 161. See also *Fortune,* February 1973, 33-34; *Business Week,* March 31, 1973, 40-41.

22. Quoted in *Business Week,* September 22, 1973, 43.

23. *Ibid.,* 52.

24. Chase Manhattan Bank, *Business in Brief,* April 1973. See also Edward Herman, "Do Bankers Control Corporations," *Monthly Review,* June 1973, 12-29.

25. Morgan Guaranty Trust Company, *World Financial Market,* January 18, 1973; U.S. Congress, Joint Economic Committee, *Hearings: A Foreign Economic Policy for the 1970s,* 973; Michael Hudson, *A Financial Payments-Flow Analysis of U.S. International Transactions: 1960-1968* (New York, 1969), 7-8; United Nations, Economic Commission for Europe, *The European Economy in the 1950s to the 1970s* (New York, 1972), 61; U.S. Senate, Committee on Finance, *Hearings: Foreign Trade,* 92:1, 249.

26. For full analysis of this problem see Paul Mattick, *Marx and Keynes: The Limits of the Mixed Economy* (Boston, 1969), especially chapters 11, 14, 15. See also Leonhard Campbell and Robert Shue, "Military Transactions and the U.S. Balance-of-Payments," *Survey of Current Business*, February 1972, 22-28; December 1972, 34-57; May 1973, 13; *International Herald Tribune*, August 16, 1973; *World Financial Markets*, January 18, 1973, 1; *Wall Street Journal*, December 21, 1972; *The Banker* (London), April 1973, 360.

27. *New York Times*, September 28, 1973; *International Herald Tribune*, November 23, 1971.

**Chapter Four**

1. As examples of innumerable studies, see Angus Maddison, *Economic Growth in the West: Comparative Experience in Europe and North America* (New York, 1964), and also his *Economic Growth in Japan and the USSR* (New York, 1969), Lawrence Klein and Kazushi Ohkawa, eds., *Economic Growth: The Japanese Experience Since the Meiji Era* (Homewood, Ill., 1968).

2. United Nations, Economic Commission for Europe, *Economic Survey of Europe 1965* (Geneva, 1966), 76-77; *Business Week*, December 12, 1970, 63; Martin Schnitzer, *East and West Germany: A Comparative Economic Analysis* (New York, 1972), 14.

3. Ernst & Ernst, *Italy: A National Profile* (January 1971), *passim*; Jossleyn Hennessy, Vera Lutz, and Giuseppe Scimone, *Economic 'Miracles'* (London, 1964), 176-84.

4. Maddison, *Economic Growth in Japan*, 50, 70; Robert Guillain, *Japon: Troisieme Grand* (Paris, 1969), 152-55; *Business Week*, April 21, 1973, 40.

5. Paul Mattick, *Marx and Keynes* (Boston, 1969), 69.

6. First National City Bank, *Monthly Economic Letter*, May 1973, 10. See also Joyce and Gabriel Kolko, *The Limits of Power: The World and the United States Foreign Policy, 1945-1954* (New York, 1972), chapter 23; Maddison, *Economic Growth in the West*, 162; Guillain, *Japon*, 22-23, 238; Murata Goro, "Greater East Asian Co-Prosperity Sphere Once Again," *Ampo*, March 1972, 17-18; Maddison, *Economic Growth in Japan*, 69; National Planning Association, *U.S. Foreign Economic Policy Through the 1970s: A New Approach to New Realities* (Washington, 1971), 8; Yutaka Matsumura, *Japan's Economic Growth 1945-60* (Tokyo, 1961), 367-445; Chitoshi Yanaga, *Big Business in Japanese Politics* (New Haven, 1968), 261-72.

7. United Nations, Economic Commission for Europe, *The European Economy From the 1950s to the 1970s* (New York, 1972), 23. See also U.S. Department of Commerce, *Overseas Business Reports*, December 1970, 20; July 1971, 20; U.S. Bureau of the Census, *Highlights of U.S. Export and Import Trade*, August 1967, 124-25; George H. Hildebrand, *Growth and Structure in the Economy of Modern Italy* (Cambridge, 1965), 79; Ernst & Ernst, *Italy*, 23; Maddison, *Economic Growth in the West*, 53.

8. First National City Bank, *Monthly Economic Letter*, May 1973, 11.

9. Hildebrand, *Growth and Structure*, 396; Vera Lutz, *Italy: A Study in Economic Development* (London, 1962), 328. See also U.N., *The European Economy*, 1-6; Maddison, *Economic Growth in Japan*, 52.

10. *Business Week*, January 13, 1973, 35. See also *German International*, January 1971, 27-30; *Monthly Labor Review*, June 1972, 32.

11. *Economist*, November 6, 1971, 80. See also Hennessy, Lutz, Scimone, *Economic 'Miracles,'* 28-57; Lutz, *Italy*, 34.

12. Guillain, *Japon*, 173; National Planning Association, *U.S. Foreign Economic Policy*, 9; U.N., *The European Economy*, 6; *Business Week*, March 31, 1973, 94-95.

13. *Economist*, August 13, 1966, 632. See also Institute of German Industry, *Economic Report from Germany*, May 10, 1967, 3.

14. *Economist*, March 11, 1967, 943. See also *ibid.*, January 14, 1967, 146; *ibid.*, March 18, 1967, 1059-60.

15. *Economist*, March 11, 1967, 943; *German International*, December 1970, 37; *Business Week*, July 7, 1973, 57.

16. Hildebrand, *Growth and Structure*, 88-89; Lloyd Saville, *Regional Economic Development in Italy* (Durham, 1967), 100.

17. Guillain, *Japon*, 312. See also Murata Goro, *Ampo*, 16; Charles Levinson, *L'Inflation Mondiale et les Firmes Multinationales* (Paris, 1973), 159; Mark Dayen, *Integrating Japan into the Free World Economy: The American Effort, 1948-1958* (unpublished manuscript, 1973), 108-09; *Monthly Economic Letter*, May 1973, 8.

18. Fritz Berg, "Germany's Economic Scene in Perspective," *Economic Report from Germany*, November 22, 1967. See also *German International*, April 1971, 25; United Nations, Department of Economic Affairs, *Economic Survey of Europe 1966* (Geneva, 1967), 1.

19. *German International*, April 1971, 25; *Washington Post*, October 14, 1971; Hildebrand, *Growth and Structure*, 79-81; U.N., *The European Economy*, 13, 23; *International Herald Tribune*, October 1, 1971; *Business Week*, May 8, 1971, 34.

20. Guillain, *Japon*, 311. See also *ibid.*, 238; *Federal Reserve Bulle-*

*tin,* April 1970, 323; Maddison, *Economic Growth in Japan,* 67; Prue Dempster, *Japan Advances: A Geographical Study* (London, 1967), 281-86; Oriental Economist, *Japan Economic Yearbook 1972* (Tokyo, 1973), *passim.*

21. Quoted in *International Herald Tribune,* June 21, 1973. See also U.N., *The European Economy,* 6-7; Maddison, *Economic Growth in Japan,* 54; U.S. Congress, Joint Economic Committee, *Hearings: A Foreign Economic Policy for the 1970s,* 91:2, Pt. 5, September-October 1970 (Washington, 1970), 984; *Wall Street Journal,* May 5, 1971; John Earle, *Report on Italy* (London, 1972), 10-11; *International Herald Tribune,* June 12, 1973; *Business Week,* January 13, 1973, 35, 39; *German International,* October 1972, 29; *Wall Street Journal,* September 19, 1973, *Le Monde,* May 8, 1973; U.S. Department of Labor, Bureau of Labor Statistics, *News,* April 6, 1973.

22. Quoted in R. W. Revens, "New Approaches to the 'New' Worker," *OECD Observer,* December 1972, 13. See also *Le Monde,* June 1, 1973.

23. Quoted in *International Herald Tribune,* June 23-24, 1973.

24. *New York Times,* September 20, 1973.

25. *German International,* October 1972, 23.

26. Quoted in *Business Week,* January 13, 1973, 35.

27. *Vision,* March 15, 1972, 21. See also *International Herald Tribune,* June 8, 1973; *German International,* July 1972, 30; Robert Ball, "Volkswagen," *Fortune,* March 1972, 82-85; *German International,* October 1972, 29; *ibid.,* April 1971, 25.

28. *Business Week,* February 5, 1972, 52.

29. *Ibid.,* 55. See also *International Herald Tribune,* June 8, 22, 1973.

30. Quoted in *International Herald Tribune,* July 28-29, 1973. See also *Business Week,* March 10, 1973, 53.

31. *Business Week,* June 10, 1972, 33. See also *ibid.,* September 23, 1972, 45.

32. *Business Week,* July 7, 1973, 59. See also *International Herald Tribune,* June 12, 1973; *Business Week,* March 10, 1973, 53; September 9, 1972, 48; November 13, 1971, 56; *International Herald Tribune,* July 14-15, 1973; *Business Week,* November 4, 1972, 38; *Wall Street Journal,* December 12, 1973.

33. Quoted in *New York Times,* November 26, 1972. See also Wilton Wynn, "Montedison," *Fortune,* March 1973, 75; *Le Monde,* October 7, 1971; *Wall Street Journal,* January 11, 1972; Earle, *Report On Italy,* 10; *Business Week,* July 7, 1973, 59; *New York Times,* March 8, 1973; *International Herald Tribune,* May 29, 1973.

34. Quoted in *Business Week,* April 7, 1973, 42.

35. Quoted in *Wall Street Journal,* April 27, 1973.

36. Joint Economic Committee, *Hearings: A Foreign Economic Policy,* 967.

37. *Business Week,* March 31, 1973, 40. See also *Wall Street Journal,* May 5, 1971; *International Herald Tribune,* June 23, 1971; *Business Week,* March 10, 1973, 53; *ibid.,* March 24, 1973, 54; *Le Monde,* May 13-14, 1973.

38. *International Herald Tribune,* May 29, 1973. See also *ibid.,* May 30-June 1, 1973; *New York Times,* October 8, 1973; *International Herald Tribune,* August 4-5, 1973.

39. Quoted in *Washington Post,* March 1, 1973. See also Guillain, *Japon,* 189-90.

40. Quoted in *Wall Street Journal,* October 19, 1973. See also *International Herald Tribune,* May 18, August 14, 1973; *Monthly Economic Letter,* May 1973, 10-11; *New York Times,* January 4, 1974; *Pacific Basin Reports,* January 2, 1974; Murata Goro, *Ampo,* May-June 1972, 55.

41. See C. D. Cohen, *British Economic Policy 1960-1969* (London, 1971), 167-96, 207-62; Susan Strange, "The Meaning of Multilateral Surveillance," in Robert W. Cox, ed., *International Organization: World Politics: Studies in Economic and Social Agencies* (London, 1969), 233-34; Leonard A. Jackson, "Exchange Control — A Stance for the Market," *The Banker,* January 1973, 33-38; *New York Times,* September 7, 1973.

42. Sidney Dell, *Trade Blocs and Common Markets* (New York, 1963), 58-59, 148; *Business Week,* June 10, 1972, 33; Kolko, *The Limits of Power,* chapters 16 and 17; *Le Monde,* January 14, 1972; *Wall Street Journal,* October 6, 1971; *Le Monde,* December 24, 1971; *International Herald Tribune,* January 15-16, 1972; Ernst & Ernst, *Italy,* 20.

43. *Wall Street Journal,* March 8, 1973. See also Kolko, *The Limits of Power,* chapters 16 and 17.

44. Quoted in *Le Monde,* January 14, 1972. See also *Le Monde* (weekly English selection), October 21, 1970

45. Quoted in *Wall Street Journal,* October 28, 1970. See also *ibid.,* May 18, 1971; *Business Week,* July 7, 1973, 58; *Wall Street Journal,* February 1, 1973.

46. Quoted in *Wall Street Journal,* October 28, 1970.

Chapter Five

1. As examples of such studies see Jagdish Bhagwati and Richard S.

Eckhaus, eds., *Foreign Aid: Selected Readings* (London, 1970); Neil H. Jacoby, *U.S. Aid to Taiwan: A Study of Foreign Aid, Self-Help and Development* (New York, 1966).

2. James P. Grant, "The Coming Marginal Man," *Business and Society Review*, Autumn 1972, 40. See also *Finance and Development*, March 1972, 29; *Ceres* (FAO Review), November-December 1972, 13.

3. *Ceres*, November-December 1972, 13; Lester B. Pearson, Chairman, Commission on International Development, *Partners in Development* (New York, 1969), 32-36, 58-62; United Nations, ECAFE, *Economic Survey of Asia and the Far East 1971* (Bangkok, 1972), 22-40; *New York Times*, January 16, 1972; Gavin W. Jones, *Implications of Prospective Urbanization for Development Planning in Southeast Asia*. Southeast Asia Development Advisory Group Papers (New York, n.d.).

4. *Ceres*, November-December 1972, 13.

5. James Grant, in U.S. Congress, Joint Economic Committee, *Hearings: A Foreign Economic Policy for the 1970s*, 91:2, May 1970 (Washington, 1970), Pt. 3, 617-18. See also U.N. *Economic Survey of Asia, 1971*, 30; Grant, "The Coming Marginal Man," 39; Erich H. Jacoby with Charlotte F. Jacoby, *Man and Land: The Fundamental Issue in Development* (London, 1971), 99, and *passim*; *Ceres*, September-October 1972, 69-70; Irv Beller, "Latin America's Unemployment Problem," *Monthly Labor Review*, November 1970, 5; *Le Monde*, June 7-8, 1972.

6. Pearson, *Partners in Development*, 20.

7. Grant, "The Coming Marginal Man," 40; David C. Cole and Princeton N. Lyman, *Korean Development: The Interplay of Politics and Economics* (Cambridge, 1971); Jacoby, *U.S. Aid to Taiwan*; U.S. Senate, Committee on Foreign Relations, *Hearings: Multinational Corporations and United States Foreign Policy*, 93:1, July 18-August 1, 1973 (Washington, 1973), 276; Gerhard Breidenstein, "Capitalism in South Korea," in Frank Baldwin, ed., *Without Parallel: The American-Korean Relationship Since 1945* (New York, 1974); Noam Chomsky and Edward S. Herman, *Counter-Revolutionary Violence: Bloodbaths in Fact and Propaganda* (Andover, Mass., 1973), 13-14.

8. U.S. Congress, Joint Economic Committee, *Foreign Economic Policy*, Pt. 3, 680-81; Gabriel Kolko, *The Roots of American Foreign Policy* (Boston, 1969), 72; *Business Week*, May 6, 1972, 90; Pearson, *Partners in Development*, 74, 272; U.S. Senate, Committee on Foreign Relations, *Hearings: U.S. Participation in*

*ADB and IDA*, 93:1, November 19, 1973 (Washington, 1973), 44-45.

9. Subimal Mookerjee, in *Finance and Development*, March 1972, 6, 9.

10. Ernest Sturc, "Fund Activities in Developing Countries," *Finance and Development*, March 1972, 3, 5.

11. Gunnar Pomasson, "Indonesia Economic Stabilization, 1966-69," *Finance and Development*, December 1970, 49. See also Pearson, *Partners in Development*, 337-45; Cox, *International Organization*, 42-43.

12. James H. Weaver, *International Development Association: A New Approach to Foreign Aid* (New York, 1965), 124.

13. Quoted in *New York Times*, September 25, 1973. See also Strange, "Meaning of Multilateral Surveillance," 335; *New York Times*, September 17, 1973; Jacoby, *Man and Land*, 142-46.

14. Raymond Vernon, *Manager in the International Economy* (Englewood Cliffs, New Jersey, 1968), 171. See also *New York Times*, September 28, 1973.

15. Pearson, *Partners in Development*, 119. See also Michael Hudson, *Super Imperialism* (New York, 1973), chapter 6, for a definitive discussion of the U.S. Government PL-480, Food-for-Peace programme; Strange, "Meaning of Multilateral Surveillance," 238, 243.

16. Harold B. Malmgren, "Coming Trade Wars? (Neo-Mercantilism and Foreign Policy)," *Foreign Policy*, Winter 1970-71, 128; *Le Monde*, September 14, 1971; United Nations, *World Economic Survey, 1969-1970* (Geneva, 1971), 137-42, 152; *Survey of Current Business*, March 1973, 46; James Petras, "U.S. Business and Foreign Policy," *New Politics*, Fall 1968, 75; Charles Levinson, *L'Inflation Mondiale et les Firmes Multinationales* (Paris, 1973), 122; *Wall Street Journal*, September 20, 1973; Teresa Hayter, *Aid as Imperialism* (London, 1971).

17. *Business Week*, April 7, 1973, 21. See also Malmgren, "Coming Trade Wars," 128; *Wall Street Journal*, May 5, 1971; *Ceres*, September-October 1972, 53; *Business Week*, November 3, 1973, 35.

18. Sidney Dell, *Trade Blocs and Common Markets* (New York, 1963), 182. See also U.N., *World Economic Survey, 1969-1970*, 143,146; Pearson, *Partners in Development*, 81; Chase Manhattan Bank, *Outlook for Energy to 1985*, June 1972; Richard S. Pedersen, "American Foreign Policy in a Shifting Setting," *Department of State Bulletin*, October 2, 1972, 374.

19. *Oil and Gas Journal*, September 4, 1967, 74. See also *ibid.*, September 11, 1967, 39; Kolko, *Limits of Power*, 446-47, 459-61;

Cora Shepler and Leonhard Campbell, "United States Defense Expenditures Abroad," *Survey of Current Business*, December 1969, 43.

20. *Oil and Gas Journal*, April 28, 1969, 33.
21. *Oil and Gas Journal*, February 2, 1970, 72.
22. Quoted in *International Herald Tribune*, July 9, 1973.
23. *New York Times*, September 20, 1973.
24. *Wall Street Journal*, November 16, 1971.
25. *New York Times*, November 5, 1972.
26. *Business Week*, March 31, 1973, 29; *Wall Street Journal*, September 21, 1973; *Business Week*, June 30, 1973, 56-63; *New York Times*, November 5, 1972; *Le Monde*, August 1, 1972.
27. *Pacific Basin Reports*, August 15, 1973; *New York Times*, November 5, 1972; Kolko, *Roots of American Foreign Policy*, 50-55.
28. *New York Times*, January 16, November 5, 1972; *Wall Street Journal*, November 16, 1971.

**Chapter Six**

1. Eldridge Haynes, "What U.S. Bankers Should Know About the USSR," *The Bankers Magazine*, Summer 1972, 32. See also Kolko, *The Limits of Power* (New York, 1972), chapter 13.
2. *U.S. News and World Report*, January 8, 1973. See also *Business Week*, July 15, 1972, 23; *New York Times*, December 10, 1972.
3. *Oil and Gas Journal*, November 13, 1972, 98. See also *International Herald Tribune*, June 9-10, 1973; *Pacific Basin Reports*, April 1973.
4. Quoted in *New York Times*, January 14, 1973.
5. *Pravda*, October 21, 1972, in *Current Digest of the Soviet Press*, November 15, 1972, 16.
6. Haynes, "What U.S. Bankers," 35.
7. Quoted by Sterling G. Slappey, "Russia: The Curtain Rises on a New Trade Era," *Nation's Business*, November 1972, 57.
8. *Ibid.*, 61. See also *Commerce Today*, April 2, 1973, 32.
9. Haynes, "What U.S. Bankers," 31. See also *Business Week*, November 18, 1972, 20.
10. Quoted in *International Herald Tribune*, June 1, 1973. See also David Rockefeller, "An Eastern European Diary," *New York Times*, February 25, 1973.
11. Willis C. Armstrong, "A New Era for East-West Trade," *Department of State Bulletin*, December 25, 1972, 723. See also *International Herald Tribune*, June 19, 1973; *New York Times*, October 24, 1973; *Commerce Today*, October 30, 1972, 40-41,

are only a few examples of the innumerable and continuing reports of trade and investment negotiations and agreements.

12. Haynes, "What U.S. Bankers," 35. See also *New York Times*, January 14, May 16, 1973; *Business Week*, January 1, 1972, 26; Charles Levinson, *L'Inflation Mondiale et les Firmes Multinationales* (Paris, 1973), 130-34.

13. Armstrong, "A New Era for East-West Trade," 723-25.

14. Kenneth Rush, "U.S. Policy Towards Eastern Europe: Affirmative Steps," *Department of State Bulletin*, April 30, 1973, 537.

15. Slappey, "Russia," 54.

16. *New York Times*, January 14, 1973. See also *Soviet News* (published by the Soviet Embassy in London), October 10, December 5, 12, 1972; *Le Monde*, June 17-18, 1973; Armstrong, "A New Era," 724.

17. Rush, "U.S. Policy Towards Eastern Europe," 537.

18. Quoted in *Business Week*, May 20, 1972, 48. See also Kolko, *The Limits of Power*, chapter 13; Herbert E. Meyer, "Why the Russians are Shopping in the U.S.," *Fortune*, February 1973, 66-67; *New York Times*, January 14, 1973; Evsei G. Lieberman, "Economic Methods and the Effectiveness of Production" in *Problems of Economics*, October 1971, 1-180; N. Petrakov, "A Market Economy for the Soviet Union?" in *Novy Mir*, translated in *Atlas*, February 1971, 22-25; U.S. Congress, Joint Economic Committee, *Compendium of Papers: Soviet Economic Prospects for the Seventies*, 93:1, June 27, 1973 (Washington, 1973), 318-22, 512-13, *passim*.

19. V. Kotov, "Prices: The Instrument of National Economic Planning and the Basis of the Value Indices of the Plan," *Problems of Economics*, May 1973, 51. See also J. Wilczynski, *Socialist Economic Development and Reforms* (London, 1972).

20. *Soviet News*, April 17, 1973, 176-78; *International Herald Tribune*, June 5, 1973; *New York Times*, November 12, 1973, January 12, 1974; *Wall Street Journal*, November 20, 1973.

21. Quoted in *Wall Street Journal*, February 2, 1973.

22. *Ibid.*

23. Robert G. Kaiser and Dan Morgan in *Washington Post*, December 28, 1972; *ibid.*, December 26, 1972; P. Khromov, "Scientific and Technical Progress and Labor Productivity," *Voprosy ekonomiki*, 1972, No. 2, translated in *Problems of Economics*, July 1972, 46-59; K. S. Karol, "Gierek's Poland," *New Statesman*, December 25, 1970; Karol, "Workers' Power in Poland," *New Statesman*, February 5, 1971, 173-74; K. F. Cviic, "Poland and the

Aftermath of the December Crisis," *Contemporary Review*, April 1971, 173-78.

24. For the most perceptive discussion of the contradictions in the Soviet system, see Paul Mattick, *Marx and Keynes* (Boston, 1969), chapters 20 and 21. Also Wilczynski, *Socialist Economic Development, passim*.

25. Michael Kaser, "Exchange and Interest Rates of IBEC," *International Currency Review*, November-December 1973, 17-19.

26. Quoted in Jean Ross-Skinner, "The Russians Are Coming," *Dun's Review*, August 1972, 88. See also *Washington Post*, December 28, 1972; Levinson, *L'Inflation Mondiale*, 134; Ross-Skinner, "The Russians Are Coming," 35-36; Wilczynski, *Socialist Economic Development*, 305-23.

27. Quoted in *Washington Post*, December 28, 1972.

28. *Pacific Basin Reports*, July 15, 1973, 152; *Wall Street Journal*, February 2, 1973; *New York Times*, September 22, 1972; *Washington Post*, December 28, 1972.

29. *Latin America*, May 4, 1973, 138-40; *International Herald Tribune*, February 23, 1972; Levinson, *L'Inflation Mondiale*, 131.

30. Marshall Green, "Trade in the Context of United States Relations with the People's Republic of China," *Department of State Bulletin*, October 30, 1972, 493.

31. *Ibid.*, 491.

32. *Washington Post*, January 19, 1973; *Business Week*, March 18, 1972, 28; April 7, 1973, 38.

# INDEX